The Coaching Conversation

Taking Your Coaching Skills to the Next Level and Impacting Lives

Authors

Carole Cowperthwaite-O'Hagan, RCC[TM]

Antoinette DuBois-Ayers, CPCC, RCC[TM]

Tim Ursiny, Ph.D., RCC[TM]

Contents

Preface

For me (Antoinette DuBois-Ayers), it all started at a dinner in 1998, with one of my good friends and her husband, a psychologist. She and I had met working at the same Fortune 100 Company, where she worked in the legal department and I was part of the finance department. Since then, we had both moved on but kept in touch for the typical post-employment *"thank goodness we left...did you hear"* gossip that keeps former co-workers bonded.

Consciously trying to include her husband, I turned to him at one point and blurted out, "Hey, what do you think about these corporate psychologists popping up everywhere?" I went on to tell them that the CEO of my new company had one and the company grapevine was having a field day with it. To add insult to injury, we had just heard his direct reports had all been assigned time with "THE Corporate Psychologist" as well. It was at this time that I discovered that my friend's husband (Dr. Tim Ursiny) had recently moved from working in private practice to now focusing on executives and teams around the psychology of performance and communication. Little did I know then that just a few years later, Tim and I would connect again and work together as coaches and trainers. Soon afterwards, we were joined by Carole Cowperthwaite-O'Hagan, another former corporate executive turned coach. Eventually, we created the Corporate Coach Program (CCP) to help both internal and external coaches increase their skills and maximize their impact. This book represents some of the training involved in that program.

The profession has evolved greatly over the last 20 years (we no longer call ourselves Corporate Psychologists, but rather Corporate or Executive Coaches) and yet the core of coaching continues to remain relevant today; we help people excel and become better problem solvers versus solving the problem for them. We hope you enjoy learning these coaching practices, whether for your own personal development, as a start to a future career in coaching, or simply to take your own coaching skills to the next level.

Introduction

While coaching has taken on many definitions, models, and approaches, in this book, we will break our discussion down into three primary areas: *What is Coaching, Coaching Skills, and Coaching Tools/Perspectives.*

Initially, coaching became mainstream during the tumultuous corporate times in the mid 1990's when mergers and acquisitions were commonplace. It transitioned with the 2008 financial crisis and the ongoing changes in the healthcare industry and has been expanded to multiple countries. While it has evolved with the times, there are some constants that have stayed true. At its core, coaching incorporates a simplistic and yet impactful approach to productive conversations. With technology whizzing by us like the speed of light, it's critical that organizational needs are consistently addressed through good communication. Organizations want an approach that aligns with corporate core values, core competencies and numerous other communication requirements within professional environments. Our approach is to focus on honoring the standards set in organizations with a coaching model that integrates those values, particularly as multigenerational teams and innovation activities take greater precedent in the workforce. That said, given that coaching is a highly unregulated field, we do believe there is confusion in the workplace about coaching. Therefore, in our first section we will give you OUR answer to the question, **What is Coaching?**

In the second section of this book we introduce **Coaching Skills**. These core skills for communication and coaching will be broken down into multiple concepts with useful exercises.

In addition, in a time when conversations occur through so many different media (in person, via phone, video conference, email, text, etc.), we'll discuss how to adapt these skills to various situations. Then we'll discuss how to incorporate these skills into our professional lives in a meaningful way, taking into account how many directions and initiatives employees are already being expected to address in their work environments.

The final section provides **Coaching Tools/Perspectives** specifically used in professional environments to assist with positive accountability and achieving results. The goal here is to provide tools that will enhance conversations, planning and goal achievement. The tools have a range of objectives, including helping people more effectively deal with emotions in the workplace and promoting clarity and direction in common areas addressed in professional environments. Those can include such areas as career growth, blocks, work/life balance and time management.

How to Use this Book

This book is designed for you to read, reflect and practice coaching skills in your professional environment. We recognize readers will choose different ways to utilize this information depending on your style, experience with coaching and current needs. That said, we encourage you to practice the exercises along the way while they are fresh in your mind after reading. If you read the book without doing the exercises, you will greatly lessen the impact of the learning.

This book is based on the Corporate Coach Program (CCP). This certification program features a two-day in-person component as well as follow-up coaching. The CCP was created for experienced professionals who want to gain more knowledge about coaching and sharpen their coaching skills. Both internal and external coaches have been certified through the program and while we taught them, we also have learned from them. This book is appropriate as a follow-up reinforcement to the course or for those considering the certification course and wanting to know more. It is also appropriate for those who are not interested in certification, but simply want to grow in their ability to coach.

Consider the following approach to receive the most benefit from this book:

1. Read – Spend time really understanding the concepts.

2. Practice – Follow the exercises to practice the concepts that were taught in the chapter to enhance your skills in that area.

3. Apply – Explore how the learning might be integrated into your professional routine.

We'd like to share one final note before you get started. Internal and external coaches refer to the individuals with whom they work using different terminology, such as clients or coachees. For the sake of consistency we will be using the word "coachee" throughout the book.

Section I: What is Coaching?

Chapter 1: Introduction to Coaching

Story

From the time I was a counselor at church camp as a teen, all I ever wanted to do was to be a therapist (from this point on we will simply use "I" to represent any of the authors). And yet, I was never fully comfortable with the idea of diagnosing people and working from a dysfunctional model. I had much more interest in positive psychology and the ability to work from peoples' strengths to maximize their potential and help them get the results they wanted to get out of work and life.

One day in 1997 I met a woman who described herself as a coach. My immediate first thought was, "What sport?" But I could tell that she was describing something different and far more interesting to me. As she described her work, my spirit got more and more excited. Coaching, as she described it, took the best of my old world, helping people and impacting lives, but left the parts behind that did not match my personality. As I embarked on multiple coaching skills training classes, I discovered that all the skills were very similar to those of being a good counselor, such as your ability to do deep discovery, listen, reflect, care, and work for the person's development. The main difference, at least from how I was trained as a psychologist, was how you viewed the person; they are not necessarily dysfunctional, they are simply blocked. They are not lost and needing your guidance; they are talented and just in need of some focus. They are not in desperate need of your wisdom; they need to reach inside and find their own answers. They don't need you to tell them what to do, but they do benefit from you holding them accountable to their goals. I found this new mindset refreshing, recharging and one that motivated me to start Advantage Coaching & Training. I have not had a single regret since.

Overview

In our over 20-plus years in this field we continue to see an ongoing thirst in professional environments for coaching. It is centered on the need for productive conversations and relationships that increase efficiency, growth and performance with individuals and teams. Organizations understand that these conversations are the foundation for building strong relationships, enhancing project progress and dealing with communication obstacles inherent in people and organizations.

Today we see coaches specializing in many areas ranging from health and wellness coaches to career coaches, finance coaches and personal life coaches. It's hard to keep them straight. In this book we focus on what it means to coach inside of a professional organization, which is what we call "Corporate Coaching." This is sometimes confused with Executive Coaching, which can also be done inside of professional organizations. However, rather than focusing **only** on an individual in a senior position, corporate coaches focus on individuals and teams who may be at any level.

The Coaching Conversation

Our Definition of Corporate Coaching:

A relationship with a willing individual which creates an environment of respect, safety, challenge, and accountability, and also motivates both the coach and coachee to achieve extraordinary results. This relationship is heavily focused on active listening and questioning to help the coachee strategize and problem-solve challenges.

As we look at this definition, you might ask, "What's different about a coaching relationship versus other professional relationships?" One of the first differences is that coaching is a relationship with a willing individual. This means that both coach and coachee have agreed to be equal parts of a coaching relationship. In other words, if the conversation is only agreed on by one party or is a one-sided conversation, it is not considered coaching. This often happens in corporate environments when someone higher on the corporate ladder meets with a direct report to discuss a particular issue in which the employee may or may not have interest but in which he/she is required to participate.

Some organizations erroneously bring in "Corporate Coaches" to fix performance issues or concerns and try to sell it to the employee as coaching. While it does provide an opportunity for the coachee to be introduced to the concept of coaching, if the coachee ultimately is not willing to participate, it is not a coaching relationship. However, if these two parties agree on a coaching relationship, mutual respect is established and a coaching relationship can begin.

The Coaching Conversation

In our experience, most people are willing to participate once they understand the benefits of a coaching relationship. I remember one particular time when an organization brought me in to coach a manager who had been assessed as "demeaning, aggressive and disrespectful". He was a talented performer and the organization wanted to keep him, but he was increasingly becoming a risk to the organization and they were on the verge of letting him go. Reaching out to an external coach was the last effort at saving this manager. When I walked into the manager's office his arms were crossed, there was a scowl on his face and he was obviously not happy to be meeting with me. So I asked, "How do you feel about meeting with me today?" and here is how the rest of the conversation went:

Coachee: This is a complete waste of my time!

Coach: So what prompted this meeting?

Coachee: It was that stupid 360 evaluation!

Coach: Please tell me about it.

Coachee: They gave it to my boss, my peers and all of my subordinates and the results came back basically saying that I'm a disrespectful bully!

Coach: So is there any truth to that?

Coachee: **No** (raising his voice, I guess to prove that he wasn't aggressive)!

Coach: That's interesting. So if there is no truth to the assessment results, what is the real issue?

Coachee: You want to know the real issue (again raising his voice)?

Coach: I really do.

Coachee: The real issue is that I'm surrounded by idiots!

Let's stop and reflect here. This gentleman obviously does not seem coachable. He sees everyone else as the problem and is not taking any initial ownership. That said, in our experience we have found that most people are coachable if you can discover their motivation for change. So what would motivate a person like that? Threat of his job was not motivating. Recognition did not seem to mean much to him. His motivation? Results. He was a dominant individual who just wanted to reach the goal no matter what. I discovered this with the use of my next question.

Coach: So what's going on with the idiots (not a word I use, but I wanted to use his language)?

Coachee: They have no sense of urgency, they don't return my emails promptly, and they are incredibly passive-aggressive!

Coach: You seem like a guy that likes to get things done. I'd imagine that is quite frustrating.

Coachee: It's incredibly frustrating. Drives me crazy.

Coach: (After a short pause). If I could help you change the way they react to you, kick up their responsiveness and get them to row in the direction of your vision, would you want to work with me?

Coachee: Absolutely (moving from anger to excitement)!

The Coaching Conversation

We worked together for six months. After another six months I contacted him to see how he was doing and was pleased to find out that instead of being fired, he had actually been promoted. He was still known as a hard driver, but had learned that a more respectful style actually got better results. Telling him that he had to be a nicer guy would have never worked. Helping him get better results by being a nicer guy was highly effective. So, as I mentioned earlier, most people are willing if you work from their motivation.

We have spent a lot of time on the word "willing" so let's move to other aspects of the coaching definition. Respect is key to having an effective coaching engagement. As you form the coaching relationship, it's important that both parties discuss and decide what mutual respect looks like for them, which is also a difference from a traditional hierarchical professional relationship. In coaching, the coachee co-creates with the coach key ground rules for the relationship, including confidentiality, the focus of their work together, meeting logistics and accountability. Today, many coaching relationships are part of development and growth efforts in which coachees volunteer or self-initiate these relationships.

In addition, coaching relationships challenge both the coachee and the coach to excel outside of their comfort zones while reaching new limits. The coaching relationship provides space and time to discuss areas for which the coachee would like to grow which requires action and accountability. Accountability in coaching is defined by both the coach and coachee and is a key component to the coaching conversation. In chapter six we spend more time on the topic of positive accountability.

Listening, another coaching differentiator, is paramount to coaching and one of the most difficult components of coaching to master. Coaches learn early on that listening is not the same as hearing and that a good listening session will inevitably lead to more questions, which will in turn, lead to more listening, and so on. You will learn more about listening in Chapter eight.

Coaching is designed to empower an individual to self-discover. Coaching at its best also moves a coachee from self-discovery to willingness to problem solve. Ideally, a coach will combine both challenge and support to help the individual continue to grow toward their potential. This reinforces the empowerment and, frankly, motivation to continue to move through the process. This process sometimes moves forward like a dance between the coach and coachee and continues moving individuals to address blocks and take action toward the goals they envision. While the coaching conversation is different from coachee to coachee, there is an art and process we'll learn in detail as we progress through the book. In keeping with this initial focus of understanding coaching, let's talk about who we would work with as a corporate coach.

Who Do You Coach?

Deciding on who you coach may depend on whether you are an internal (employee) coach or an external coach. External coaches, of course, could coach anyone within an organization. This is seen as one of the benefits of working with an external coach. In this type of relationship, typically position and rank are irrelevant. External coaches may work directly with the coachee or may contract with the organization. Internal coaching may be informal or official where assignments are from within the organization. Informal coaching means two individuals have decided to work with each other without any specific direction from the company. In official relationships, we typically see organizations that want to promote a culture of coaching by assigning coaches to employees.

In the best organizations, you see coaching in multiple directions:

- Peer-to-peer coaching

- Manager-to-subordinate coaching

- Coaching up (yes, even subordinates coaching managers)

There are multiple benefits and blocks to multi-level coaching. For instance, coaching peer-to-peer can be naturally comfortable in a familiar environment. Peers typically understand the culture and objectives. This allows for space for them to listen, support problem solving and serve as an easily-accessible accountability partner. However, peer-to-peer coaching may be ineffective when colleagues are not willing to listen or hold each other accountable.

Manager-to-subordinate coaching requires the manager to consider the context of the conversation. In most cases, coaching can be effective when working with subordinates. Some of the benefits of coaching as a manager include the subordinate's involvement in decision making, taking ownership, providing input to plans, and being involved in the vision. The challenge for managers is to know when it is important to manage and when it is important to coach. For example, when mission critical situations arise and an immediate decision needs to be made, managing may be the preferred method.

What is not often considered is coaching up. We encourage coaching up when the manager is receptive, desiring the coaching and has good professional boundaries. However, these parameters are not always present, so judgment is needed for each particular corporate culture and individual. The potential dangers are power imbalances that can happen when the relationship is already strained due to power struggles. This approach may also be inappropriate when confidentiality around corporate issues may restrict open coaching. Coaching up, however, can be extremely effective when the manager is new in their role, or new to the organization, or new to a particular situation and the direct report has established themselves as a trusted advisor while respecting the appropriate lines of authority.

Practice/Exercise

Let's take a minute to reflect on the best coach you have ever had, the coach in your life who had the most impact on you. It could be a sports coach from childhood, a person in your professional life that has helped you with your career (mentor, boss, colleague), or a friend or family member who has coached you well in life.

The Coaching Conversation

Once you have that person in mind, think about characteristics that made that person stand out to you and list them below.

My Best Coach_____

Characteristics of my best coach (the skills, abilities, characteristics that made this person a great coach):

_____

_____

_____

_____

_____

_____

_____

You may notice from your list the two sides represented in coaching. We refer to them as the soft side and the hard side. The soft side includes characteristics similar to encouraging, great listener, empathetic, caring, and trustworthy. The hard side represents characteristics such as holding your feet to the fire and challenging you to get out of your comfort zone. A good coach has both sides. We find most people are naturally good at one side and need to work to strengthen the other side.

Neither is better than the other. In fact, one without the other creates imbalance in coaching. If you focus on the soft side *only,* you run the risk of coachees not achieving their results in a timely manner and merely having a friendship. If you focus primarily on the hard skills, then you may receive early results but might not create the safety for the other person that would allow them to admit fears, mistakes or blocks that need to be addressed in order for them to grow and develop. A good coach first understands which area comes naturally to them and then learns to strengthen the other side.

Envision this analogy: let's say you are working out at the gym and specifically working on your biceps with dumbbells. Most people have one side that is naturally stronger or more limber than the other side. Does that mean we only work the side that is easier? Of course not! How many people want to consciously build one bicep larger than the other? So, just as we want symmetry in our bodies, we want to be balanced in our coaching approach to provide the full scope of results.

Question: Which side (soft skills or hard skills) comes most naturally to you?

My _____skillset is the side which comes naturally to me.

   (soft/hard)

My _____ skillset is the side which I can work on strengthening.

    (soft/hard)

Application

Based on what you have just learned, answer the following questions.

    1. Where in life do you think you have been an impactful coach?

    2. What are your coaching strengths?

    3. What specific abilities could you develop to become an even better coach?

Quote

"When I dare to be powerful, to use my strength in the service of my vision, then it becomes less and less important whether I am afraid."

— Audre Lorde

Chapter 2: Understanding Coaching

Story

It was actually my son's interest in soccer, specifically the Fédération Internationale de Football Association (FIFA) and the World Cup, that drew my interest to Iceland. Amongst other things, they have created a reputation for themselves as a soccer powerhouse. However, as I investigated further, I learned that Iceland is trendy not only because of soccer but because of some other unique facts. If you Google Iceland you will find all kinds of fun facts, such as:

- The Icelanders' telephone directory is organized alphabetically by first name.

- It's considered inappropriate to address anyone by Mr. or Ms.

- Almost all Icelanders use the first name with everyone, including the president of Iceland.

- Roughly 85% of Iceland's energy is from renewable resources, and well over half of that is geothermal alone.

- 95% of Icelanders believe in elves.

As interesting as all of these facts may be, what is catching the world's attention at the time of this writing is their national soccer team. In 2018, Iceland, with a population of 335,000, was the smallest nation ever to qualify for the World Cup. Much to the disbelief of many Americans, including my son, the USA did not qualify. Just one year earlier, Iceland had become the 33rd ranked team in the world, rising a full 100 points from 133rd in 2012. This was done in an unprecedented five short years.

Besides the fact that the country is small and people believe in elves, soccer fans (and leadership coaches) from around the world are watching them with a close eye to see what they are doing to create such rapid success. In a *60 Minutes* interview, they attributed their success to creating a vision, committing to a goal, identifying various paths, creating a plan and tracking progress, while tweaking along the way. In other words... coaching.

In theory this sounds simple. Any champion athlete will tell you, the plan is the easy part; execution is the killer.

Overview

In this chapter we are talking about coaching and the core beliefs that help people and organizations reach remarkable goals. We will also discuss unique characteristics about corporate coaching that help organizations to succeed. Finally, we'll discuss the differences in coaching and other common roles in professional organizations.

Core Beliefs about Corporate Coaching

In general, coaching has core beliefs that guide the approach and methodology. We share these with coachees during the discovery phase to establish an understanding. As compared to traditional management, some of these may align and others may be very different. We have six that have served as an informative and yet simple introduction to coaching.

The Coaching Conversation

1. **The coachee is capable and creative.**

   As coaches and managers, we believe the people we are coaching are smart and capable of learning and that they are creative in their own way and have their own ideas on how to progress with their goals.

2. **There is greater motivation when the coach connects with the coachee's agenda.**

   Helping a person to self-discover is far more powerful than having someone tell them what to do. We are guided by the theory of Socrates: *there is power in asking questions.* This allows coachees to answer questions or choose where they may seek the answers. When we encourage people to think about, voice and create solutions, they are invested in the results in a personal way. People don't destroy what they create.

3. **A coaching relationship requires mutual respect, trust, and honesty.**

   For coaching to be successful, the relationship must be open, genuine and respectful. Also part of developing a great coach/coachee relationship is looking inwardly and assessing strengths and challenges. One way we like to look at these strengths and challenges, specifically in the area of trust, is by completing a Trust Assessment (shared later in this chapter).

4. **A coach aids a coachee in overcoming obstacles to success.**

A coach notices and identifies patterns for their coachee and addresses them directly when they consistently run into blocks to success. Most people have some obstacles to success, such as fear of success, procrastination, and lack of confidence. Normalizing and finding the right way to help a coachee address these is key to a successful coaching engagement. Later in the book, we will introduce a variety of tools that will help coachees identify and overcome blocks.

5. **Coaches encourage self-direction and excellence.**

   Coaches encourage their coachees to seek out answers and solutions in a personalized way while challenging status quo and habitual ways of thinking and acting. With a coach, individuals tap into a level of excellence, of which the coachee may or may not be aware. The relationship encourages them to go further and grow faster than they would on their own.

6. **Coaches help coachees be accountable and move to action.**

   Every coaching session includes action steps and accountability. There are various ways to include these in a coaching session. Coachees become familiar with the expectation and come to their sessions prepared to move out of current comfort zones in order to achieve goals. Each coachee is different, and a coach adapts to asking questions in a way to determine the balance between movement and overload.

The Coaching Conversation

Uniqueness of Corporate Coaching

In corporate coaching, we need to remember that we have two coachees; the person we are coaching and the organization that is funding the coaching. It is unethical to ignore either coachee! Therefore, in corporate or executive coaching, both the organization's and the individual's goals are important. Neither should be sacrificed for the other. The question of confidentiality is often raised at the beginning of a coaching engagement. Ideally, we prefer to have complete confidentiality concerning the details of the coaching engagement with the exception of the coaching goals and how invested the individual is in their coaching. The most important thing is that the level of confidentiality is decided upon in advance and that all parties are in agreement to the boundaries of information sharing.

This invariably brings up the issue of an employee who, during their coaching, decides to leave the organization. We believe that soon after, if not at the moment of making a firm decision to leave, the individual should start paying for their coaching out of their own pocket. However, we do not believe that it is the coach's role to inform anyone of the coachee's decision. That is the responsibility of the coachee.

While this may be a sensitive issue for an organization that invests in coaching with the intent of retaining the coachee, we also believe that coaching a person who decides to leave an organization will often aid the organization. If the coachee's heart and focus are not in their current position, then the organization suffers too. Helping the coachee create an amiable exit strategy that not only benefits the coachee, but also helps set the organization up for success, is far more beneficial to an organization than keeping an unhappy employee. Helping a coachee self-select to leave an organization also avoids damaging legal battles in the future.

Differences in Coaching and Other Interactions

It is not uncommon for our corporate coachees to compare coaching to therapy due to the very personal nature of the interaction. We like to say that while coaching is not therapy, it can be therapeutic.

Coachees often get confused between the differences in consulting, coaching, managing, therapy and mentoring. While it seems like each of these professional services overlap to some degree, they maintain their own unique value and are each valuable in the right setting and circumstance.

Consultants, for example, are typically hired to bring in expertise in a specific area. Like coaches, they usually start an engagement by asking a lot of questions, and good consultants are usually good listeners. However, soon after their interviewing, their expertise comes into play and they provide solutions in their specific chosen area. Having good listening skills and providing an objective opinion is valuable, but is usually different from coaching in the level of challenge to the coachee and in holding them accountable to behavior change.

Therapy and coaching can seem similar at first because the skillsets between a therapist and coach have quite a bit of overlap. That said, therapists are usually hired for their expertise in mental health, diagnosing disorders and prescribing treatment, including referrals to psychiatrists or general practitioners if medication is necessary. Coaches do not diagnose, nor do they consider the role of medication. Also, in general, coaches spend very little time discussing the past and have a primary focus on the future and specific goals held by the coachee. While venting may be part of coaching, coaches are not working to heal your past. They are focused on creating your future. That is why there are occasions where a coach may be working with an individual who is also concurrently seeing a therapist.

Mentoring is a term that often is used interchangeably with coaching and, while similar, is also distinctly different. Mentors, unlike coaches, are seasoned professionals who are experts in a specific profession where they have years of experience. Coaches, while potentially experts in their former professions, are not hired for their industry or position specific expertise, but rather their expertise in human dynamics and bringing out the best in others. In fact, coaches who have no working knowledge of their coachee's profession often are more disciplined in staying in the Socratic Method to bring out their coachee's expertise. In general, someone chooses a mentor because they have walked the path, and the individual wants to hear their stories and understand how they navigated to their level of success. A mentor MUST have expertise in the subject area. A coach does not need expertise in the subject area and can work with individuals in fields in which they have never personally had experience.

Managers, unfortunately, are often asked to wear some version of all of these hats. However, they are hired first and foremost to ensure the success of the organization. Success for a manager is driven through managing their staff, which may at times include consulting with them, listening to their challenges, mentoring them on how to navigate through the company, and coaching them toward their goals. However, managing is usually not pure coaching because the manager has specific dictates and goals determined by the company, and is responsible for ensuring that his or her team meets these specific goals.

In coaching, the coachee is the expert on how, when and where they want to proceed to reach a goal. With the help of the coach, they define how they will be most successful in moving forward with a solution. The coach listens, guides, encourages, challenges and co-creates the goals that keep the coachee on track. In coaching, the coachee is the expert on the **how**; the coach is expert on the **process**.

Practice/Exercise

Here is an example of a coaching tool that you might use on yourself or with a coachee to help him or her self-assess their different trust tendencies. After completing the exercise we will briefly discuss how a coach would address the results in comparison to how a mentor would address the results.

In this exercise, we use the acronym **TRUST** (Tolerance, Reliability, Understanding, Self-revealing and Truthful), to determine an individual's strengths and areas for improvement as it relates to this important factor in human relationships.

The Coaching Conversation

For each of the following, rate how well you do in demonstrating that aspect of trust.

Tolerance – I show patience and acceptance of others even when we disagree.

5	4	3	2	1
Very much so	Mostly	Somewhat	Slightly	Not at all

Reliability – I keep my agreements and follow through on my commitments in a timely fashion.

5	4	3	2	1
Very much so	Mostly	Somewhat	Slightly	Not at all

Understanding – I show empathy and care for others and what they are going through; I am caring in my feedback to them.

5	4	3	2	1
Very much so	Mostly	Somewhat	Slightly	Not at all

Self-revealing – I let others get to know the "real me" and am genuine with my feelings and thoughts.

5	4	3	2	1
Very much so	Mostly	Somewhat	Slightly	Not at all

Truthful – I am straightforward and truthful with others even when it is difficult.

5	4	3	2	1
Very much so	Mostly	Somewhat	Slightly	Not at all

The Coaching Conversation

Assessing your score

Obviously the closer you are on each scale to the "5", the greater trust you are likely to build with others and your coachees. Let's look at each in a little more detail.

Tolerance – It is difficult to trust someone when we feel judged by them. We tend to trust people more when they accept us and are able to disagree with us without judging.

Reliability – We trust people who are dependable. If you over-promise and under-deliver, then trust can be impacted.

Understanding – How well do you empathize with others? How well are you able to put yourself in their shoes and understand their experiences? We trust people who "get us" emotionally.

Self-revealing – When I talk with you am I getting your genuine self? We tend to be suspicious when people keep things close to the vest, hiding what they feel, think or do.

Truthful – Will you give me honest feedback? Are you straightforward? We do not trust people who talk behind our backs and won't be genuine with us.

If you were mentoring someone after completing this assessment then you would share stories from your experience of how you addressed each of these trust components. You would give them ideas of how they could grow and emphasize the role of trust in your success. If you were coaching the person, you would ask questions to help them see the impact of these trust components on their life and work. You would help them gain insights on personal tendencies that impact trust and guide them to develop approaches to leverage the trust components that were strengths and tactics to help overcome their more challenging trust behaviors.

Application

In this section, we have defined corporate coaching, who you coach, and beliefs about coaching in professional environments. Ask yourself these questions as you consider applying these concepts in your environment:

1. Where in your professional environment could coaching be helpful?

2. What current beliefs do you have around managing vs. coaching and what beliefs could be revised to be even more helpful?

3. In what circumstances would coaching be difficult in your professional environment?

Wrapping up this chapter, we go back to our story about Iceland soccer. Ultimately, to what does the Iceland soccer empire attribute their rapid success? As we said, coaching! But let's be more specific.

- Every coach in Iceland gets paid (from youth on up).

- Every coach is professionally trained.

- There are no amateur coaches, whether it is coaching a four-year-old team or a professional team.

- Every kid who plays pays an annual fee and can train with a professional club.

Imagine the pipeline of players this is creating! Coaching works.

Quote

"An idea that is developed and put into action is more important than an idea that exists only as an idea."

– Buddha

Chapter 3: The Coaching Conversation

Story

I have to say rock climbing has never really been on my bucket list; however, apparently it was on my daughter's! One winter, while living in Chicago, my daughter asked me if we could head over to the health club and take on the climbing walls. I agreed, thinking it would be a good way for HER to stay active. When we went there, it was evident that she was a natural, scurrying up the kiddy walls as if she was skipping down a sidewalk. Soon she moved on to much more difficult climbs.

It was only a matter of time before she convinced me to try it. Not as brave as she is, I opted for the kiddy wall. There I was, sweating it out, using the kiddie handles of butterflies, turtles, etc., and frankly proud to make it a third of the way up, even if kids were giggling as they passed me.

This went on for a number of visits until I eventually graduated to making it HALF-WAY up the kiddy wall. Woo hoo!!! I was feeling pretty proud, despite the fact that my legs were shaking, my hands were tired, I was afraid to look up or around and especially down. I was also starting to feel self-conscious with my 50-year-old rear end up there. So, having pushed myself just enough, I decided to head back down. That's when I heard a voice that sounded like it was from the sky. "Mom! Mom! You're doing it! You're almost there!"

The Coaching Conversation

I was thinking, "What, is she crazy? I already beat my best, I feel good and I'm getting down from here."

"But Mom, you don't have much further to go." So I mustered the courage to glance in the direction of her voice. She was up in the very corner of the room; she had just scaled the wall with no grips and had turned around to watch me from the top. She began telling me to just put one more foot up to the yellow banana, "It's right there, Mom, you can do it!"

I yelled back, "No, I'm scared and tired and my legs are shaky."

"But, Mom, you are so close." I did as she instructed. Next, it was to grab the panda ear and then step on the leaf, and so on. She continued with genuine encouragement. "Look, there's a blue fish you can grab, and put your foot on the snail. You're doing it! Just two more."

I was still scared, but she was there guiding and encouraging me as I asked her which grips to choose. I didn't agree with all the recommendations, but I realized how nice it was having someone invested, encouraging and helping me with my blocks. "Just one more, Mom!" And then, "You did it!!!! I knew you could do it."

I was so relieved when I got down that it took me a while to realize what a great coach she had been to me while having this conversation.

The Coaching Conversation

Overview

The term "Coaching Conversation" refers to a specific way of interacting with another person with the goal of bringing out their absolute best. While specific and structured, it also represents a very comfortable and natural form of interaction. At the same time, like the wall-climbing conversation, it may not always be comfortable since your coach may be stretching you out of your comfort zone. In this chapter, we will explore the Corporate Coaching Conversation Model, noting that while predictable in flow, it is not stiff or regimented. In fact, as we walk through this, you will see how the non-linear approach allows the coach to engage and shift the conversation to suit the coachee.

Incorporating the core values and beliefs from the previous chapter, we use a 5-step model in the Coaching Conversation. Having a model gives direction and routine to a process that is otherwise varied depending on the individuals, their situation and a host of other factors. So, taking into account that every coaching relationship is unique, this model provides a simple and yet thorough approach to guide you through your coaching conversations. For each phase in the conversation, we will walk you through the purpose, the execution and the application.

The 5-Step Coaching Conversation Model

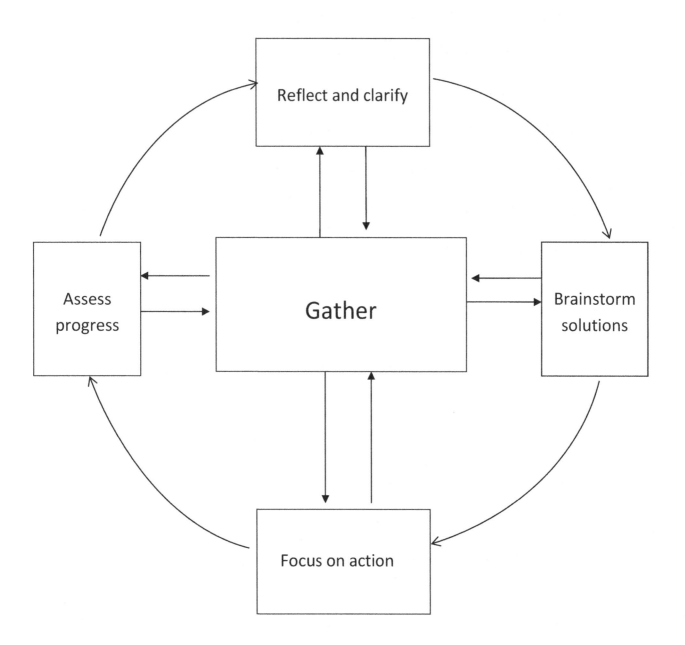

Phase 1: Gather

Purpose:

The Gather phase is basically about doing your deep discovery on the issue, the challenges and the motivation. We gather information and emotions in coaching to get to know the coachee and understand them. In this phase we open up the conversation, collect information about what is important to them, understand how they feel about the situation, assess their level of motivation for change and keep their ideas and perspectives in the forefront. Additionally, it allows the coachee to set the agenda in each session, zeroing in on where they would like to take the meeting and what would be most useful in the moment. For example, a coach might be working with a coachee on a long-term strategic initiative and suddenly the coachee finds they are dealing with a customer service issue that needs immediate attention. Honoring the gathering phase, the coach will switch gears and align the conversation with the coachee's immediate need (when appropriate and desired) and return to the greater focus when the coachee is ready to move on.

Below are the skills used during the Gather phase. Each one builds on the other to create an understanding of the coachee's goals, blocks and talents for reaching their potential. In section two of this book we unpack each of these skills in detail.

Execution:

- Ask powerful questions (see Chapter 5)

- Listen

- Pace your presentation; essentially match non-verbal intensity, rate of speech and body language as long as you don't appear aggressive or passive

- Collect all relevant data, perspectives and feelings

- Utilize the power of observation; trust your instincts and notice the feelings the coachee is exhibiting (excitement, fear, anxiety, willingness or boredom); check in on these; it's all part of the coaching and gathering phase

Application:

The Gather phase is integral to the rest of the model. It is the support system in moving forward in the coaching conversation. Having this foundation creates an understanding of our coachee's wants and needs.

Phase 2: Reflect (Clarify)

Purpose:

During the Reflect phase, the coach is paraphrasing, summarizing and verbalizing what he or she is hearing from the coachee. This, of course, requires focused listening skills and the ability to synthesize what the coachee is verbalizing. The purpose of reflecting is to create a bond with the coachee, demonstrate that you are listening and to make sure you are tracking correctly in the session.

Sometimes when we paraphrase back to the coachee we realize that we have actually misinterpreted what they were saying. Other times it simply makes them feel good that the coach is connected to them or generates additional thoughts and perspectives as they hear their own words reflected back to them. This creates a connection and an environment that fosters growth, safety and motivation. When a coachee feels connected to their coach they can be vulnerable as well as empowered, which opens the gates to self-discovery.

Execution:

We connect by:

- Listening

- Paraphrasing, summarizing and clarifying

- Reflecting both emotions and content of what they are saying (remember that verbalizing your understanding of what a coachee is saying does not mean that you agree; you are simply showing that you have heard their perspective)

- Returning to the Gather phase as you continue to grow in your understanding of the issues, challenges and goals

- Agree on the anticipated results

Application:

Reflecting and building a connection with the coach is the glue that holds the coaching relationship together. In the anticipation of going after goals it can easily be overlooked or bypassed. Before moving into problem solving, this is where we do a mental check, pause and reflect, to ensure that the coach and coachee are on the same page. When the coach feels like the issues are fully understood and the coachee is motivated to address the challenge, then it is time to move to Phase 3.

Phase 3:   Brainstorm Solutions

Purpose:

Once you understand and have connected with your coachee, you can move into brainstorming solutions and ideas. This takes the innovation side of coaching to its greatest heights, where the coachee is free to explore without judgment. We frequently hear from coachees that when they dedicate time to this phase, it is a freeing process that typically does not occur in their busy schedules on a regular basis.

Phase 3 allows for unrestricted space to problem solve. In the purest form of coaching, the coachee is the one doing the brainstorming while the coach continues to ask powerful questions to both generate new ideas and to use discernment to critique ideas that are being generated. Many newer coaches feel the temptation to jump in and solve the problem for the coachee. While not inappropriate as a form of helping another person, it can rob the coachee of the chance to solve their own issue and grow as a problem-solver. It's like going to a personal trainer. Can you imagine working with a

personal trainer who lifts all the weights for you? They would be robbing you of your

chance to build your muscles!

Execution:

- Work through blocks to achieving goals

- Use their motivation for change

- Ask powerful questions to help the coachee brainstorm multiple possible

  solutions

- Help the coachee self-critique their ideas so that they are able to determine the

  best approaches

- Return to the Gather and Reflect phases as needed

Application:

Brainstorming is a phase of coaching that can vary quite dramatically from coachee to

coachee. Some coachees have endless ideas and strategies while others struggle with a

starting point. Here's where the coach identifies these differences and proceeds

according to their coachee's needs. With both situations, we support the coachee in

clarifying their vision. With coachees who have many ideas, the coaching begins to

narrow down their priorities to prepare for the next phase. For coachees who struggle,

it is a good time to look at what blocks may be in their way (see chapter 10). No matter where the coachee is, this phase encourages them to open up, stretch into new directions and think outside the box.

Once the coachee has brainstormed a significant number of quality ideas, it is now time to move to Phase 4.

Phase 4: Focus (Move)

Purpose:

It is the Focus phase that most clearly differentiates coaching from a typical conversation. Now the information and tactics, which were self-discovered previously, are compiled to create an action plan. Again, through questions and reflection, the coachee creates a plan for moving forward. As with previous phases, the coach checks in to determine the coachee's commitment, direction and overall support in completing their action steps.

Execution:

- Move the conversation to action
- Create and implement an action plan

Application:

Summarizing the discussion, areas of importance, success parameters and discussed tactics are key in this phase. This supports the coachee in developing an action plan for which they can be accountable. The plan must be measurable and individualized. Doing a final check-in on the coachee's motivation and level of commitment will uncover any apprehension and/or provide an opportunity to refine the action to support their success. The coach's role is to be clear, using SMART goals (Chapter 4) for the coachee's next step. While Phases 1 – 4 can be done in a single meeting, Phase 5 occurs in the next interaction between the coach and coachee.

Phase 5:   Assess (Measure)

Purpose:

In the previous phase coachees agreed to be held accountable to an action plan that is measurable. The Assess phase is about following up on that plan to celebrate success of progress and to problem-solve any blocks to the plan's execution. It deepens the relationship with the coachee knowing someone is invested in their commitment and their success. This accountability raises the stakes in completing the action item. While coachees are never shamed for the lack of completion of action steps, they are held accountable to either reassess the importance of the actions or to overcome the blocks to the execution of their plan.

Execution:

- Measure progress against goals

- Maintain accountability and movement

- Look for next level progress

- Walk the line between full acceptance of the coachee (not expecting perfection) and challenging them to overcome obstacles to their success (encouraging progress)

Application:

Following up on action items is a regular part of the coaching conversation. This occurs at the beginning of the next appointment. The coach asks the coachee what worked, what didn't work, and how the coachee feels about completing or not completing each action item. This learning will set the stage for establishing new action steps for the following call. The assessment phase is often what encourages coachees to persevere on a goal that has not shown progress. Once the Assess phase is completed, the coaching conversation goes into Phase 1 again to address the goals and opportunities for the current coaching meeting.

Using the Model

As mentioned earlier, coaching is not a linear process. Like other conversations, it has components, in this case the five phases. However, as with all conversations, it can go in a multitude of directions. There are key pieces that separate a coaching conversation from a general conversation. One is the agreement to move forward with an action. The action may take all shapes and forms (tasks, research, thinking, etc.). All coaching sessions begin with a check-in from the previous session and wrap up with an action item. The other elements are weaved throughout the conversation depending on the topic being discussed. It is important that the coach remains the guardian of the conversation to make sure that it is always productive for the coachee.

Another key piece to note in utilizing the model is that the coachee is doing the work in each phase. For example, in the Brainstorming part of the process, you are not brainstorming; rather, you are aiding the coachee to brainstorm.

Finally, while some people may argue about the Gather phase being at the center, we believe that connecting and observing are significant skills necessary for a capable coach. The truth is, none of these stages can be successful without the other and the coach needs to be able to verbally "dance" with the coachee. Coaches must be in constant observation of the coachee's response to questions, nonverbal language, and statements and be able to "flow" with the coachee. They must note reactions, hesitancies, and energy levels. Powerful questions without observational skills and reflection are merely an interview or an interrogation. Coaches recognize the power of all phases in the Coaching Conversation model.

Practice/Exercise

Review the following coaching interactions. As you read through them, think about the Coaching Conversation model and what phases are included or excluded in the conversation. Envision in your mind the difference between these two coaching conversations:

The Coaching Conversation

Sample of an Ineffective Coaching Session

Notice how the coach uses directive questions or statements and doesn't allow the coachee to brainstorm.

Tony: I have a communication problem. I am struggling with a person on my team. Her name is Lisa.

Coach: Did you talk to her?

Tony: That's what my boss wants me to do but I don't feel his advice helps and actually it makes me feel even worse.

Coach: You should tell him he's not being helpful.

Tony: I guess I can try to talk to her. I just need to figure out what I will say.

Coach: Don't you think it would be a good idea to tell her that you are struggling with her and make the request that she change the way she is communicating with you?

Tony: Ok...I'll do that.

Coach: Good luck and let me know how it goes.

While a bit artificial, we have actually seen this kind of interaction from brand new coaches in our training sessions!

Sample of an Effective Coaching Session

While we have truncated the conversation for the purpose of space, notice the coach's use of questions and how the coach is able to move the coachee through the process without having to know any of the specific details.

The Coaching Conversation

Tony: I have a communication problem. I am struggling with someone on my team. Her name is Lisa.

Coach: Tell me more. [GATHER]

Tony: I feel Lisa from my team is always taking charge and telling people, including me, what to do.

Coach: How does that make you feel? [GATHER]

Tony: It makes me feel like a subordinate when I'm actually her manager.

Coach: Sounds frustrating. [REFLECT]

Tony: It really is; I think it makes me look bad to the rest of the team.

Coach: What do you think will happen if this continues? [GATHER, while building motivation for change]

Tony: Well, a couple of things. I think it will hurt morale on the team, get in the way of us collaborating together and make me look like a weak leader.

Coach: Sounds like the impact on both you and the team might be pretty damaging. [REFLECT]

Tony: Absolutely. I really need to address this.

Coach: How specifically would you like Lisa to change? [GATHER]

Tony: I would love to see her listen more to others' ideas, actually find value in those ideas and be a little more diplomatic in how she shares her perspectives.

Coach: So if you were able to get her to listen better, value other perspectives and improve in how she communicates her own ideas, how would that impact you and the team? [GATHER and REFLECT combination, again building a vision and motivation for change]

Tony: We would work together as a team to solve problems rather than feeling frustration when she steps in.

Coach: What have you done so far to address the situation? [GATHER]

Tony: I have certainly hinted to her that she could be nicer in how she communicates, but I've done it in a very light-hearted, almost joking, fashion.

Coach: What was the impact of that kind of approach? [GATHER]

Tony: Ha! I guess I was fooling myself, because it didn't have any impact whatsoever.

Coach: Given that a light-hearted approach doesn't work, what might be a better way to address this? [REFLECT and BRAINSTORM]

Tony: I think that she needs a more direct approach, but I should still show respect for her thoughts and perspectives.

Coach: So what would that more direct approach look like? [REFLECT and BRAINSTORM]

Tony: Well, it would have to be both respectful and crystal clear.

Coach: What would you say? [BRAINSTORM]

Tony: I would approach it from the angle of asking her how she thinks the team could work better together and use that to open the door for me to provide her with feedback.

Coach: As you give her feedback, what specific requests do you want to make of her? [BRAINSTORM]

Tony: I will ask her to be more encouraging of other team members and verbalize value to both their ideas and mine, just as I do, and will continue to do, with her ideas.

Coach: So after asking for her thoughts and addressing those, you would give her specific feedback on her impact on you and the team and make the request for more encouraging and positive communication. As you hear yourself share that aloud, what do you think? [REFLECT and GATHER and moving into FOCUS]

Tony: I think that conversation is long overdue and needs to happen.

Coach: By when do you want to have that conversation? [FOCUS]

Tony: Before our next meeting.

Coach: Fantastic. I look forward to speaking with you next Thursday at 10:00 am at our next scheduled time. [ASSESS at the next call]

Tony: Sounds like a plan. Thanks!

In a full coaching conversation we would likely go even deeper in the tactics and help the coachee prepare for difficulties and challenges in the conversation, but the above example at least gives you a sample of how the coaching conversation might flow. Dealing with conflict is also more fully addressed in Dr. Ursiny's books, *The Coward's Guide to Conflict* and *The Top Performer's Guide to Conflict*.

Practice/Exercise

A good way to practice this model is to work with a partner and practice dialoguing different scenarios. Keep the model in front of you and practice longer conversations where you might move in and out of different phases, coming back to the center, GATHER, each time you think the coachee might have more information to offer in the conversation.

Application

Using the model:

1. Use this model in a current challenge in your professional environment to explore multiple solutions. How did this model assist in creating new ideas?

2. Choose a conversation in your professional environment that could have had a better outcome. How would using the Coaching Conversation model make a difference?

3. Practice, practice and practice. After each interaction, assess yourself on how well you stayed disciplined to the model. How well did you ask powerful questions? How accurate were your reflections? How well did you allow the coachee to do the brainstorming vs. doing the heavy lifting for them? How effectively did you focus the conversation on action? How well did you do in creating positive accountability in the Assess phase?

Quote

"Coaching is unlocking a person's potential to maximize their growth."

– John Whitmore

Section II: Coaching Skills

Chapter 4: Setting Goals

<u>**Story**</u>

Laura had recently been promoted to branch manager due to her success as the top sales producer for the company. She was respected by her direct reports and worked hard to push the team to achieve their goals. When it came time for her annual review, she was confident that her boss would be pleased with her team's financial success, but was caught off guard when he rated her low on her ability to delegate and to grow members of her branch. She assumed that being a leader meant making sure her team reached their numbers. Instead, what she learned is that while making the numbers is highly important, if she wanted to continue to advance within the company, she would be expected to develop her leadership skills. Her boss rated her as stellar on being a problem-solver, but low on her ability to mentor and grow others into becoming great problem-solvers. This was a different skill set and one that Laura had never focused on before.

Laura and I worked together to identify different areas of growth on which she could focus to become a great leader. We coached on her ability to set a captivating vision, align people with that vision, and hold her subordinates accountable in an empowering way that would lead to their personal development and growth. This involved understanding her current skill set, identifying where she needed to improve, and then building a plan using the SMART goal methodology to create action steps. Laura gave this new challenge the same focus and energy she gave to becoming a great producer and her next review showed tremendous progress.

Overview

In this chapter we will discuss SMART goals as a universally accepted approach to goal setting. We have found in our corporate work that team and organizational goals give individuals the ability to home in on their vision and stretch in new ways.

While goal setting is linked to higher rates of success, according to an article on a <u>Harvard Business Study</u>[1], goal setting is not a standard practice among individuals. According to the study:

- 84% of the population does not have goals

- 13% have a plan in mind, but have unwritten goals

- 3% have written goals

The study went on to find that the 13% who have goals are 10 times more successful than those without goals. The 3% with written goals are 3 times more successful than the 13% with unwritten goals. Goal-setting in writing is obviously a powerful tool in the coaching process.

---

[1] Sid Savara, "Why 3% of Harvard MBAs Make Ten Times as Much as the Other 97% Combined," https://sidsavara.com/why-3-of-harvard-mbas-make-ten-times-as-much-as-the-other-97-combined/

The Coaching Conversation

One of the universal goal-setting strategies that has been around for some time is represented by the acronym SMART. This strategy can be used for a variety of scenarios, including employee performance, project deadlines, and personal development. The SMART goals system is embraced in the workplace because of its simplicity. While there are some variations in what each letter represents in different organizations, below are the steps we use to make sure that goals are SMART.

Specific - Define the goal in a clear and concise way. What exactly do you want to work on? What do you want to achieve?

Measurable - Determine how you will quantify your goal. How will you measure the results you want? What will you hear, see, and feel when you complete this goal?

Actionable - Incorporate movement to take your goal from point A to point B. What tasks or steps will you take to move closer to your goal? What resources can you find and utilize to progress toward your milestone?

Realistic Make sure your goal is doable and practical. How likely, on a scale from 1-10 (1 being not likely, 10 being very likely), is it that you will achieve your goal?

Timed Set a timeframe for completing your goal. How long will it take you to complete this task? How committed are you to this schedule?

Applying the SMART model to your goals provides a guide to goal setting. See below for some simple examples.

- I will be at least two minutes early to 75% of my meetings this entire month

- I will increase my sales production by 10% by the end of the fourth quarter

- I will develop a new form to track our team's progress by next week

- My department reviews will be finished by May 1st

There are many ways to start the goal-setting process. In the Practice/Exercise section we will introduce some tools we use to assist in getting started.

Practice/ Exercise

It's not uncommon for some coachees to know exactly where they want to start in coaching. They come to a coach knowing what they want and why they want it. However, others need something to help kick-start the process. This is where we use the Balance Wheels. Coachees choose to work with either the Professional or Personal Balance Wheel. We have coachees who want to grow in their work/life balance and may incorporate both wheels. As you can see, the choice is specific to the coachee.

Balance Wheels present topics in a comprehensive yet simple format. Completing these wheels gives coachees a visual from which to work. Look at each topic within the wheel separately as well as together to get a full spectrum of how other areas in life or work are impacted by each other. In professional environments, the Balance Wheel is a beneficial tool for new coaching relationships. It serves as a baseline in goal setting.

Process:

Step 1: Complete the Balance Wheels.

- Within each of the following eight areas, circle the number that best represents your level of satisfaction in that area of your life (7 = completely satisfied; 1 = completely dissatisfied)

- Connect the dots to see what the wheel looks like.

Step 2: Ask the coachee to self-reflect on the results and determine a starting place. As the coach, it is important to not assume that the lowest-scored area is the preferred starting place for the coachee. Rather, ask the coachee what stands out to them.

Step 3: Coach on the selected area and assist the coachee in creating SMART goals.

The Coaching Conversation

Professional Balance Wheel

Within each of the following eight areas, circle the number that best represents your level of satisfaction in that area of your professional life (7 = completely satisfied; 1 = completely dissatisfied):

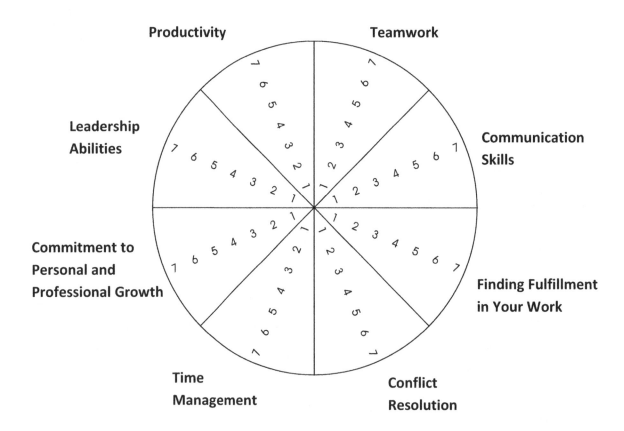

Now, connect the dots. The rounder the wheel, the more balanced your professional life.

Imagine how your car would travel if the wheels were in this shape!

The Coaching Conversation

Personal Balance Wheel

Within each of the following eight areas, circle the number that best represents your level of satisfaction in that area of your life (7 = completely satisfied; 1 = completely dissatisfied):

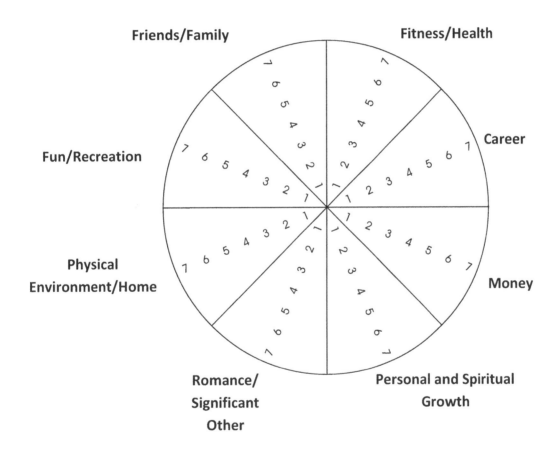

Now, connect the dots. The rounder the wheel, the more balanced your life. Again, imagine how your car would travel if the wheels were in this shape!

To take your Balance Wheel goals to the next step, you can use a tracking program to assist. There are many available online. Find the one that works for you. One we use for coachees who struggle with staying on track is the simplistic and straightforward Goal Setting and Action Planning chart below. This identifies the larger goal and breaks down key areas including start date, target date and specific action steps to achieve the goal.

GOAL SETTING AND ACTION PLANNING

Five Goals to Reach In 90 Days

What are the five goals you most want to set for yourself in the next 90 days? Please select only those goals that you really want, not the ones you should, could or might want. Look deep inside, then write down your five personal or professional goals, and discuss these with your coach. When you set the right goals for yourself, you should feel excited, a little nervous, ready and willing to go for it!   Do not select the goals you historically have chosen, but never reached, unless you are in a much better position to reach them now.

The Coaching Conversation

Start Date   Target Date   Specific Measurable Goal

Goal 1

_____   _____   _____

Action steps to reach this goal:

_____   _____   a._____

_____   _____   b._____

_____   _____   c._____

Goal 2

_____   _____   _____

Action steps to reach this goal:

_____   _____   a._____

_____   _____   b._____

_____   _____   c._____

Goal 3

_____   _____   _____

Action steps to reach this goal:

_____   _____   a._____

_____   _____   b._____

_____   _____   c._____

Goal 4

_____   _____   _____

Action steps to reach this goal:

_____   _____   a._____

_____   _____   b._____

_____   _____   c._____

Goal 5

_____   _____   _____

Action steps to reach this goal:

_____   _____   a._____

_____   _____   b._____

_____   _____   c._____

Application

We all have the ability to make choices in life. You can watch others grow, you can decide to grow, or you can wonder what happened as life passes you by. We started this chapter talking about why people set goals. Goal setting is a natural motivator and will help you achieve what you want faster than if you do not have written goals.

The achievement of goals builds confidence and encourages us to set more goals. It's an interesting cycle; the more goals you set and achieve, the more motivated you are to achieve even more goals. Goal setting also keeps people going during tough times. Short goals with quick wins give people hope during transition and difficulty. Challenging goals promote growth and learning as individuals. People who set goals actually change their outlook on their future.

Setting SMART goals and taking action is an important element of how one achieves success. The Balance Wheels presented are a simplistic and streamlined way to help assess how someone views themselves in multiple elements of life or work. These can help you or your coachees discover areas on which to work and act as a starting point to address and set a specific goal to achieve.

What is a SMART goal you want to accomplish today? Feel free to fill out one of the Balance Wheels above (Professional or Personal) with someone. Pick an area of challenge to work on and use the SMART system to create some form of action to move forward on your area of challenge. You can also have a coachee do this and guide them through the process described in this chapter and below.

1. What is a goal you have wanted to achieve personally or professionally in the past 3-6 months?

2. What is stopping you from moving forward with this goal?

3. How can you break this goal down by using our SMART system?

Quote

"If you can dream it, you can do it."

— *Walt Disney*

Chapter 5: Asking Powerful Questions

<u>**Story**</u>

Jennifer came to her coaching call one day completely out of character. By the speed at which she was talking, and the volume of her voice, she was clearly frustrated. She started to explain that she had just come from her fifth meeting of the day and this last one, in particular, was the ultimate proof that these meetings were a waste of time. She went on to paint the picture of the demise of the meeting she just attended, which she was actually supposed to facilitate.

She said, "We had 12 people in the room. Of the twelve, five had their laptops out, four were staring at their phones almost the entire time, two were without electronics and clearly upset that the others weren't paying attention. As the person running the meeting, I kept giving hints that we needed to focus, but no one was paying attention. Mind you, this meeting was a regular weekly meeting that started in January for a project that is to launch in September. Fast forward six months and we are way behind, but did we focus today? No, today's meeting was the epitome of a waste of time! Not only were most of them on their devices the whole time, but a couple brought lunch, two buddies were having regular sidebar conversations, and I swear one person was on social media half the time. I have better things to do with my time."

As Jennifer's coach it was apparent what the topic of our coaching session was going to be this day. Something was going on in the structure or execution of the meeting that had allowed bad habits and complete disinterest to develop. It also appeared as though Jennifer had been somewhat passive or timid in her facilitation approach, "hinting" that they needed to focus, but not truly taking control of the meeting. To address her frustration, Jennifer needed to find a way to get participants either reengaged in the meeting and/or set some ground rules and instructions for how the team was to work together in these meetings.

Now I could have jumped in with a lot of advice for Jennifer, but my role as Jennifer's coach was to engage her in a series of powerful questions where she could work through the issue and come up with a solution for herself. By taking her down the path of self-discovery, she would completely own the solution and grow in her problem-solving abilities. We explored questions such as:

- If this continues, what will be the consequences?

- How would you like the meeting to go?

- How might you get the team members more engaged in the project?

- What conversations have you had in the past about appropriate behaviors in the meeting?

- When someone shows distracting behaviors, what would be the best way to address that?

And so on. Soon Jennifer came up with her own solutions. She was going to take a multi-step approach to the challenge.

1. She was going to educate the group on where they were in the process and share how behind schedule they were, as well as the need to have higher focus in these meetings.

2. She was going to take ownership in front of the group that she had never set guidelines for the structure of the meeting.

3. She was going to take about 15 – 20 minutes to facilitate the group to agreement on their "rules of engagement" in the meetings.

4. If any team member continued to break the rules she would have a separate one-on-one meeting with them.

While it took a couple of attempts, eventually Jennifer got control of the meeting, turned her frustration into energy for change, and finished the project on time. She knew what she needed to do; Jennifer just needed someone to listen, ask the right questions, and hold her accountable to execute her approach.

Overview

In this chapter we learn the value of questions and what makes a question powerful. We will review what causes leaders to tell people what to do in situations where a question would be far more appropriate as well as empowering for the person. Finally, we'll introduce a series of powerful questions in a formula that provides a structure for deep discovery.

New coaches find this approach helpful in getting coaching started, as well as staying on the path to helping coachees uncover new ideas and move to positive accountability while working toward a goal. We like this description by Fran Peavey, a pioneer in the use of strategic questions. She states: *"Questions can be like a lever you use to pry open the stuck lid on a paint can. . . . If we have a short lever, we can only just crack open the lid on the can. But if we have a longer lever, or a more dynamic question, we can open that can up much wider and really stir*

things up. . . . If the right question is applied, and it digs deep enough, then we can stir up all the

creative solutions."[2]

Questions in coaching and professional environments serve many purposes. Questions invite

participation in conversations, solicit opinions, and encourage creativity. They can lead to

innovative ideas, action and change.

If we reflect on the coaching model, we use questions that allow the coach to gather

information from a curiosity perspective. Questions can explore facts, feelings, relationships

and behavior. There are questions which encourage creative thinking, others that promote self

–discovery, and still others that narrow the focus of a conversation. Once a focus is identified

there are questions that support coachees in holding themselves accountable to acting on their

ideas.

Questions not only challenge the coachee to think, they also put the coachee in the driver seat.

Questions can lead to solutions that have buy-in, passion and commitment.

---

[2] Eric E. Vogt, Juanita Brown, and David Isaacs, *The Art of Powerful Questions* (Mill Valley: Whole Systems Associates, 2003)

The Coaching Conversation

If you want assurance you are asking a powerful question, keep these simple rules in mind.

1. Ask open-ended questions. Open-ended questions open up the brain. These questions encourage more creativity, keep the conversation flowing and lead the coachee to brainstorm most effectively. If someone can answer your question with a "yes" or a "no," then it is a closed-ended question. Questions that can be answered with a "yes" or a "no" are not necessarily bad, but they do tend to have the effect of shutting down the brain. "What could you do about this challenge?" is an open-ended question that is likely to generate more ideas than the closed-ended equivalent: "Is there anything you can do about this challenge?" When you want the coachee to think, use open-ended questions. When it is time to shut down the conversation or just check on something, closed-ended questions are fine. Also, coaches need to realize that closed-ended questions such as, "Have you thought about doing _____?" are not really questions, but rather advice in disguise!

2. Start questions with who, what, how, when and where. These will assure you have an open-ended question. If you start your question with did, have, do, will, can, etc., it is a closed-ended question.

3. Understand when to use "why" questions. "Why" is also open-ended, but it needs to be used very carefully, specifically and strategically. Often people feel defensive when asked a question starting with "why." For example, "Why did you do the report that way?" "Why aren't you done yet?" "Why are you late?" These uses of "why" sound parental and judgmental. While "why" often invites defensiveness, it always invites justification. Therefore, we encourage coaches to only use "why" when you want the coachee to justify something. For example:

- Why are you excited about your vision?

- Why is that important to you?

- Why has your team been successful?

When used to reinforce something positive or motivating, it actually further reinforces their vision or overall reason for pursuing their goal.

Keeping these three simple points in mind when asking your powerful questions will open up conversations for greater coaching success.

Ten Powerful Questions

The following 10 Powerful Questions provide a useful process around your Coaching Conversation model. With time and experience, these questions will come naturally. In the meantime, they provide a practical formula and structure for walking through the coaching process. These serve as an initial base of questions.

1. What do you want?

Not "*what should you do*," but "what do you want?" Be specific. Allow the coachee to dream and question what they really desire in their work setting. Look at specific skill areas where they would like to grow that would benefit their career and the company.

2. What will achieving what you want do for you?

After the coachee answers this question, you might ask the question again. Keep asking ("what else?") until you get to the core of what the coachee really wants. This allows the coachee to understand what they are striving for. It increases motivation to achieve the goal. However, if the coachee is not excited when answering this question you might be on the wrong goal or there could be a hidden block.

3. How will you know when you have it?

Have the coachee describe what they will see, hear and feel upon achievement. Have them be specific; fill in as much detail as possible. You may ask the coachee to describe a full-length motion picture of their achievement.

4. How will others know when you have it?

Ask your coachee to describe what an outsider would see, hear and feel. What will they notice that is different about you?

5. Where, when, and with whom do you want it?

Support your coachee in having a clear context for their goal. Ask them to be specific.

6. What stops you from having it already?

With this question the coachee identifies barriers to their achievement. What areas must be handled in order to achieve their goal?

7. How will your desired outcome affect other areas of your life?

This is a question many people overlook. Have the coachee look at the wholeness of their life. How will this outcome affect their life balance in both negative and positive ways?

8. What resources do you already have that will contribute to getting your outcome?

Ask coachees to take stock of what they already have available to assist them (experience, friends, tools, etc.).

9. What additional resources do you need in order to get your outcome?

Challenge the coachee to explore what else they may need. Have them step back and be specific.

10. How are you going to get there?

People can talk all day long about what they want. This question supports the action behind the picture. Have a coachee determine a first step and use the goal setting techniques from Chapter 4 (i.e. SMART goals).

The Coaching Conversation

There are thousands of questions the coach could ask, but there is rarely, if ever, one right question. These are just ten examples that can flow naturally into action. While there are no perfect questions, we do believe that coaches should have high self-awareness of what types of questions they are asking and why they are asking those particular questions.

As a coach, you will improve dramatically by fully understanding the following five types of questions.

- FACTUAL questions: *What happened? What initiated this new project? What is the timeline? Who is included? What is the budget?*

- EMOTIONAL questions: *How did you feel about what happened?*

- BEHAVIORAL questions: *What did you do as a result of what happened? What do you plan to do?*

- RELATIONAL questions: *What role did others play in what happened?*

- SPIRITUAL questions: *How does what happened match who you are and who you want to be?*

The key to asking these questions is to wait patiently for an answer. Silence is golden in coaching. Whether you are on the phone or in person, trust that the coachee has an answer. It is okay as a coach to feel a little uncomfortable with the silence as a coachee ponders an answer. We don't have to jump in and save them with our answer. We talked about the importance of affirming and reflecting what you hear from your coachee. This is critical and quite different from giving an answer.

We will take the questions to one more level by referencing Bloom's Taxonomy (Armstrong)[3] of questions. As you advance in your coaching and questioning skills, thinking about questions from a more in-depth perspective will provide additional direction when working with coachees.

Benjamin Bloom created a classification system for types of questions. While his system is often applied in educational settings, it does provide a useful framework for determining the types of questions best asked in a coaching situation.

Level 1: Knowledge Questions – Help coachees share facts and basic concepts.

Sample Questions:

- *What is . . . ?*

- *When did _____ happen?*

- *Why did . . . ?*

Level 2: Comprehension Questions – Help the coachee organize, compare, and give descriptions of main ideas.

---

[3] Patricia Armstrong, "Bloom's Taxonomy," https://cft.vanderbilt.edu/guides-sub-pages/blooms-taxonomy/

Sample Questions:

- *How would you compare . . . ?*

- *What is the main idea of . . . ?*

- *How would you summarize . . . ?*

Level 3: Application Questions – Help the coachee solve challenges by applying knowledge, facts, techniques and rules in unique ways.

Sample Questions*:*

- *How would you solve _____ using what you have learned . . . ?*

- *What approach would you use to . . . ?*

- *What other way could you plan to . . . ?*

Level 4: Analysis Questions – Help the coachee examine and break information into parts by identifying motives or causes and making inferences.

Sample Questions:

- *What is the theme . . . ?*

- *What conclusions do you draw . . . ?*

- *What is the relationship between . . . ?*

Level 5: Synthesis Questions – Help the coachee bring information together in a new way by combining thoughts and ideas in a new pattern and potentially proposing alternative solutions.

Sample Questions:

- *What changes would you make to solve . . . ?*

- *How would you improve . . . ?*

- *How could you change (modify) the plan to . . . ?*

Level 6: Evaluation Questions – Help the coachee make judgments concerning information,

validity of ideas or quality of work based on a set of criteria.

Sample Questions:

- *How would you evaluate . . . ?*

- *How could you determine . . . ?*

- *How would you prioritize . . . ?*

Asking questions is an art. Masterful questioning not only requires the coach to listen well, but

also requires genuine curiosity. By following your coachee's response, you will quickly be able

to tell which questions are powerful and which only fill up the time.

<u>**Practice/Exercises**</u>

Exercise #1: In this exercise, practice your ability to create different types of questions. We will

give you some examples after the exercise, but don't look ahead! Try to really challenge

yourself.

Scenario: One of your direct reports comes to you complaining that she has a conflict with

another of your subordinates. Thinking about the Gather phase of the Coaching Conversation model, what open-ended questions would you ask in each of the categories? Try to keep your

answers appropriate to the Gather phase. After doing that we will do the same exercise,

focusing on the Brainstorming Solutions phase.

What FACTUAL questions would you ask to gather information?

What EMOTIONAL questions would you ask to draw out and understand their feelings?

What BEHAVIORAL questions could you ask to find out about how they handled the

situation?

What RELATIONAL questions might you ask to understand the other person's role in the

situation or additional individuals involved?

What SPIRITUAL questions would help you understand how consistent they are being with their identity and values in how they have been handling the situation?

Using the same scenario, let's develop brainstorming questions in each of the categories.

What FACTUAL questions would you ask to gather information about options for the future?

What EMOTIONAL questions would you ask to draw out and understand their feelings about the different approaches?

What BEHAVIORAL questions could you ask to find out about how they might handle the situation in the future?

What RELATIONAL questions might you ask to understand how others might react to their approach?

What SPIRITUAL questions could you ask to help motivate them to fully handle the situation, while remaining true to their identity and values?

Sample questions for each phase:

Note that many questions overlap between categories. For example, a factual question such as, "What actually happened?" could involve emotional, behavioral and relational elements.

Gather phase

- Factual

    o What actually happened?

    o What led up to this?

- Emotional

    o How did that make you feel?

    o What is your main emotion about the situation now?

- Behavioral

  - What did you do when that happened?

  - What have you done in the past when this has come up?

- Relational

  - How did she respond when you said that?

  - What impact did this have on the rest of the team?

- Spiritual

  - How does how you dealt with the situation match who you are and who you want to be?

  - If this continues, what will be the impact on your brand in the company?

Brainstorming Solutions phase

- Factual

  - What are your different options with this situation?

  - What resources do you have for addressing this?

- Emotional

  - How would you feel if you were able to empower yourself in this situation?

  - If you took that approach, how would that feel?

- Behavioral

  - What might you do about this?

  - What action makes the most sense?

- Relational

    - How do you think they will respond to that approach?

    - What will the team think of that?

- Spiritual

    - To grow as a leader, what do you want to do?

    - What does integrity dictate that you do in this situation?

Exercise #2: In your next team meeting or discussion with a colleague, notice the questions being asked and do two things:

1. Notice if the questions are open-ended. If not, how would you revise them to be open-ended? Also, how did making the question open-ended impact the discussion?

2. Notice where an open-ended question could be revised to a more curious question. How does that impact the discussion?

Application

The ability to ask powerful questions is perhaps the most important skill for a coach to master. Powerful questions lead to coachee buy-in, motivation, clarity and results!

Quote

"A question not asked is a door not opened."

– Marilee Goldberg [The Art of the Question]

Quote

Chapter 6: Creating Positive Accountability

<u>**Story**</u>

Being based in Chicago, I will admit to some biases around our professional sports teams. When I think about accountability, a player comes to mind that many in our country, and frankly around the world, have also admired - *the one and only...Michael Jordan.*

Allow me to reminisce about the era when I had Bulls season tickets at the original Chicago stadium. Our tickets were literally right behind the players. The echo, energy and excitement were beyond any experience I could describe. Boy, did I look forward to those games! Even in those days, Michael gave his "A" game through it all. I loved watching him; he had such a gift... his ability to plan, move and shoot were all intentional. He once said that his secret to success was that he demanded more from himself than any other person could expect from him. This level of accountability was truly powerful and his fans were fortunate to see him rise.

Similarly, in coaching we help our coachees be accountable for their goals. We help them build that same level of focus and determination to meet and surpass their goals. Often in a corporate environment, accountability is brought into play when someone has done something wrong: "You messed it up so I am going to hold you accountable." This is why the word accountability often comes with a negative connotation. However, when accountability is created in a positive and motivating way, it is inspiring and is something people look forward to and appreciate.

The Coaching Conversation

Overview

When you look up the word accountability you will see definitions similar to this: "The obligation of an individual or organization to account for its activities." Take it a step further and look in the thesaurus and you will find words like blame, liability, guilt, and incrimination amongst others. It's no wonder most people perceive the act of accountability in a punitive way. In this book you will notice we use the term "positive accountability." Top performers embrace accountability in a way that enhances their achievement of goals. Your ability to create positive accountability in your coachees is related to your balance between focusing on the relationship and focusing on the results. Leaders and coaches who balance these two well are able to create inspiration and innovation. Examine the following chart:

High focus on relationships

1		4	
Permissive Leads to a casual culture		**Positive Accountability** Leads to a committed culture	

Low focus on results ———————————————— High focus on results

Apathetic Leads to a chaotic culture		**Hierarchical/Authoritarian** Leads to a compliant culture	
2		3	

Low focus on relationships

The Coaching Conversation

Let's start with **Quadrant 1**. If a coaching relationship has a high focus on the relationship, but a low focus on results, the level of accountability is **Permissive**. Coachees in this environment may enjoy the relationship and enjoy their coaching, but are unlikely to grow. The coach makes them feel valued, recognized and important, but does not challenge them to be their best. This creates a nice but underperforming environment.

Quadrant 2 represents a low focus on the relationship as well as a low focus on results. What a sad situation this would be! The coach is not really focused on the relationship and is not challenging the person to do his or her best. Most, if not all, coaching relationships would not be able to survive this type of environment. We refer to this level of accountability as **Apathetic.** This can happen if a coachee is forced into coaching and has no interest in engaging.

In **Quadrant 3,** if there is a low focus on the relationship, but a high focus on results, the coach may be seen as just another boss who can shut the coachee down and make them fearful of opening up and being vulnerable. The coach pushes the person to grow, but does not create safety and recognition in the relationship. We call this a hierarchical or **Authoritarian** approach. This can happen when the coach feels pressure from the organization to change the coachee and becomes more interested in his or her own performance and reputation rather than in what is best for the coachee.

Quadrant 4 happens when there is high focus on the relationship _and_ a high focus on results. There is respect, recognition _and_ challenge in the coaching relationship which allows the coachee to feel safe stretching outside their comfort zone. It is this balance that builds trust, confidence and the ability to have healthy and tough conversations to reach new levels of problem solving. We call this **Positive Accountability** and this is where top performers reside. The best coaches create this balance for their coachee.

Accountability can be a vulnerable experience for the coachee. When accountability includes shame and judgment, the coachee can feel rejected or unsafe. In these situations, trust is challenged and the willingness to take risks is limited. The other side of this coin is when you do a disservice to your coachee by "letting them off the hook" too easily. Both approaches limit success and are disrespectful to the coachee. Positive accountability is a balance between empathy and challenge. It can be empowering if handled with respect and strength.

So what does a coach do if a coachee fails to complete his or her action steps? Well, the permissive coach would treat it as "no big deal" or work too hard to make sure the coachee feels good about themselves. The hierarchical coach would shame the coachee and try to make him or her feel guilty. The positive accountability coach would do several things. First the coach would look for any evidence of progress. Even if the coachee did not perfectly complete the actions, did he or she show progress over the past? If so, the coach would emphasize this. Focusing on progress is especially important if the coachee has a history of guilt or harmful self-expectations. Secondly, the coach would do deep discovery on what blocked the coachee from fully completing the action steps. This takes understanding some of the most common reasons that coachees fail to complete their actions. We have experienced some of the following:

- The action never was truly important to them. Perhaps they agreed to the action steps in order to please the coach. Therefore, the coach needs to discover the importance level of the activity by asking questions such as, "How important is completing this action step to you?" This discovery will either lead to reprioritizing the action step or dropping it.

- Life "got in the way." Sometimes coachees will have the best intentions, but during the weeks between the coaching sessions, unexpected events occurred that interfered with their commitments. The first time this occurs the coach usually does a quick check to make sure that no deeper blocks exist and then simply gives "grace" to the coachee. They then reprioritize the action for the next session. If, over time, the coachee shows a pattern of "life getting in the way," then the coach shifts the focus of the session to coaching on that pattern of behavior, helping the coachee discover why the pattern exists and how to break it.

- There is a hidden block that has not been addressed. Through deep discovery the coach should be able to uncover any hidden blocks. The Pain/Pleasure analysis discussed in Chapter 7 is an excellent tool for uncovering these blocks. One of the most common hidden blocks is fear of success. While fear of failure is fairly obvious, fear of success is much more insidious. Many reasons exist for fear of success.
  - Fear that they may get it and lose it (so they would rather not get it in the first place)
  - It is unknown, and often we fear the unknown
  - Concern that others will be jealous of them

- o Fear that if they hit record goals, others' expectations of them will increase

- o Feeling that they don't deserve it, especially if they came from modest means

An experienced coach will always be alert for these potential blocks to growth. There is some learning that needs to take place first. "Failure" is often simply an opportunity to learn and grow. As long as a coachee learns from their failure to complete their actions, they have opportunities for growth.

Again, coaches do not shame, but they do treat accountability seriously and with respect in order to challenge the coachee to grow.

Practice/Exercise

High focus on relationships

Permissive Leads to a casual culture	**Positive Accountability** Leads to a committed culture
Apathetic Leads to a chaotic culture	**Hierarchical/Authoritarian** Leads to a compliant culture

Low focus on results ———————————— High focus on results

Low focus on relationships

The Coaching Conversation

Using the above graph, think about people you have managed or coached in the past and ask yourself the following questions. By creating your own mental imprint, this can help guide you and get you back on track when you find your coaching relationships drifting out of Positive Accountability.

- In which quadrant do you spend most of your time?

- Which is harder for you, focusing on the relationship (showing care, recognition, connection) or focusing on results (challenging people to work to their potential)?

- If you are not in the Positive Accountability quadrant, to which quadrant do you tend to drift?

- What might be some ways to catch yourself making this drift?

- When you find yourself out of the Positive Accountability quadrant, what mantra could you use to shift back into creating positive accountability?

After analyzing yourself with this exercise, what new habits do you want to put into place to create even greater positive accountability in those you coach or lead?

Application

The creation of positive accountability is an important skill for a coach to master. When done correctly, accountability becomes a gift, not a punishment.

Quote

"It is not only what we do, but also what we do not do, for which we are accountable."

– Moliere

Chapter 7: Helping Coachees Make Decisions or Get Unstuck

<u>**Story**</u>

We had just moved to a new city in between school semesters, and acting as "responsible" parents, we immediately put our children into activities so they could meet friends. As with any big change, there was a lot to keep coordinated between traveling parents, new school requirements, new grocery stores, keeping track of kids' schedules, etc. Well, we had been in this new community about a month and on this particular day my 11-year-old son was in a spring break soccer camp. It was at the community center and his dad had dropped him off in the morning with his lunch. At around 4:30 I received a call from a neighbor, to whom I had not given my number, so panic set in immediately! She told me my son was sitting in her front yard under the tree and he couldn't get into our house. I had assumed his dad picked him up, but it quickly became apparent that we had not communicated well on the transportation schedule.

It was an hour and a half after camp ended! What happened? I asked, "How did he get there?" My neighbor said, "I don't know, he just gave me your phone number." I rushed out of the office to see what had happened. I learned that he waited patiently after camp, thinking his dad was coming to pick him up. After 30 minutes, the camp counselor, a high-schooler, told my son he needed to lock the door. So out he went. I wanted to get mad at the camp counselor's decision but knew it was best to first take care of my son and see how he was feeling about what had happened.

The Coaching Conversation

He told me he walked home. "Really? That's pretty good. How did you find your way? How did you figure it out?" We decided to hop in the car and go back to the center and have him show me step-by-step how he found his way to our new home. We started all the way from the door at the community center. He walked down a hill and near a grocery store where we shop sometimes, then went straight to the busy four-lane road, which he knew would lead to our house. Once there, he said, "It was scary. There were really loud trucks and buses coming by fast. So I looked up and saw some apartment buildings that I know Myles lived in, so I started walking that way."

As he was telling the story, we started clocking the mileage. He told me what he was thinking about on each block and what he recognized. After the first half mile he saw a friend out on the sidewalk riding his ATV. He stopped and played for a bit, but didn't tell him he was lost. He decided he better keep walking because his dad might be worried and looking for him. At the mile marker he recognized the house of another friend from school. At that point he knew exactly where he was. In about 5 or 6 blocks he reached the school.

He began to describe the relief he felt knowing where he was. He was tired, but at least the worry was gone. So he moved more quickly. He decided the walk would be easier if he put his soccer cleats in his lunchbox (it felt like less to carry). He knew he had about 15-20 minutes to get home. But when he arrived, no one was there and he was pretty thirsty. Kitty-corner across the street was a family who had a daughter the same age as his sister, so he decided to go there. He asked for water and agreed to wait outside while the neighbor mom called me.

We clocked almost two miles, and by the time he had told his story he had moved from upset to proud. What we learned and celebrated was the number of decisions he had made along his journey to get to his goal. It was so valuable to stop and recognize how he made his choices and what it yielded. He empowered himself through different decisions and recognized milestones along the way.

We make decisions at any age from youth through adulthood every day. Coaching is essentially a series of small decisions to reach a number of goals based on a vision. Decision-making varies from person to person and understanding how to help coachees make decisions wisely and efficiently is a powerful coaching skill.

Overview

What is your typical decision-making process? Whether your goal is minor or major, do you prefer to decide based on your instincts, or are you more process-driven and elaborate? No matter what you choose, decisions are part of growth, and as coaches we see our main job as helping people make conscious decisions. In this chapter we will learn about what motivates us to move forward to make decisions vs. what keeps us stuck. We will also introduce a specific decision-making tool.

In the book *The Upward Spiral*[4], we learn that neuroscience research studies show that decision-making increases happiness regardless of whether it is a good decision or not. Eric Barker[5] puts this research in context nicely when he says, *"The point is, when you make a decision on a goal and then achieve it, you feel better than when good stuff just happens by chance. This answers the eternal mystery of why dragging your butt to the gym can be so hard. If you go because you feel you have to or you should, well, it's not really a voluntary decision. Your brain doesn't get the pleasure boost. It just feels stress. And that is no way to build a good exercise habit."*

Decision-making is critical in coaching. While the traditional pro/con list can be effective to guide decisions, it focuses mainly on the logical reasons to go with one choice over another. In our experience, emotions are just as important as logic in making decisions, so we take the traditional pros and cons list a step further. Coach Tony Robbins has focused extensively on the role that pain and pleasure have in guiding our choices, so we built a simplistic way to elicit the pain and pleasure involved in any choice. Research shows that 80% of decisions are based on the pleasure that comes from the results or from avoiding a negative (pain) outcome. We utilize our Pain/Pleasure analysis when coachees are having a tough time making a decision or if they are simply stuck. Like a pro/con list, this exercise also provides a tangible visual to review and reflect on later if coachees question the decision they have made. Let's review the process.

---

[4] Alex Korb, *The Upward Spiral* (Oakland, CA: New Harbinger Publications, Inc., 2015)
[5] Eric Barker, *Barking up the Wrong Tree* (New York: HarperOne, 2017)

The Coaching Conversation

Pain/Pleasure Analysis

	Pain	Pleasure
Option #1		
Option #2		

This is an easy chart to draw. I find when I'm coaching I will draw it up quickly and have the coachee do the same on the other end of the phone if we do not have a hard copy in front of us. Here are the steps in the process:

Step 1: Define option #1 and option #2. The options should be dichotomous, such as exercise/don't exercise; delegate more/don't delegate more; go after the new job position/stay in my current role; have that tough conversation/don't have that tough conversation, etc. If the coachee knows that one of the choices is probably better for them, make that option #1. The coach helps the coachee label the two options by asking simple questions. Examples are, "What are the two opposing actions you are considering?" or "If this came down to two choices, what would those be?"

Let's use the example of delegation. Given that delegation is often an important skill for leaders to develop, we will use "delegate more" as option #1 and "don't delegate more" as option #2. The numbers in the boxes represent an order that we have found useful where "1" represents the first box you engage with and "4" represents the last. Obviously, as your coachee is talking, if they mention something that belongs in a different quadrant than the one in which you are focused, you can simply put it in the correct quadrant and then return to the current quadrant.

Pain/Pleasure Analysis

	Pain	Pleasure
Delegate more	1	4
Don't delegate more	3	2

Step #2: Ask your coachee to share the pains of option #1 (i.e., "What is a pain of delegating more?"). As they share the pains, the coach is not agreeing or disagreeing or trying to get the coachee to problem-solve the blocks, but rather is listening, reflecting back and encouraging the coachee to keep generating responses. So for example, if the coachee says that one pain is "the loss of control", then the coach would say something like, "Absolutely, that is a very common one. People are often concerned about losing control when delegating so let's put that down." Then the coach (and the coachee if over the phone) writes down the bullet point, "losing control." After that the coach would simply say, "What else?" and repeat the process until the coachee runs out of blocks. Do not write the same thing twice! So, for example, if the coachee later says, "I like to keep my hands in everything so it goes my way," the coach would simply ask, "Is that different from loss of control?" If the coachee answers affirmatively, put it into the quadrant; if negatively, then do not write it down.

Step #3: After the pain of option #1 is completed, go to the pleasure of option #2. So in this case, it would be the pleasure of not delegating. Therefore, the coach would ask, "What is a pleasure of not delegating?" If the coachee just repeats a different phrasing of a pain of option #1, such as "I get to keep control" then the coach should mention that control is already covered and we are looking for new things in this quadrant. Some of the most common answers in the pleasure of not changing are things like "easier" or "comfort zone."

Following this method, you will now have all of the blocks for option #1. It is now time to move on to the motivators.

Step #4: Cover the pain of option #2 (in this case it would be the pain of not delegating). The coach asks, "What is painful about not delegating?" and may receive answers such as, "I'm too busy," or "It is going to limit the success of the team." As in the previous quadrants, the coach listens, reflects and encourages more thought, while writing down the coachee's answers in the appropriate quadrant.

Step #5: Cover the pleasure of option #1 (delegate more) asking the coachee, "What is pleasurable about delegating more?" This quadrant will reveal all of the positive motivators for change including such potential thoughts as, "I love growing people", "I'll be able to focus my energy on more strategic activities," etc.

The Coaching Conversation

Represented below is a potential version of the completed analysis.

Pain/Pleasure Analysis

	Pain	Pleasure
Delegate more	<ul><li>Loss of control</li><li>It takes time</li><li>What if it does not go well?</li></ul>	<ul><li>Time for more strategic things</li><li>I like growing people</li><li>Better life balance</li></ul>
Don't delegate more	<ul><li>I'm too busy</li><li>It will limit our results</li><li>I'm stuck doing vs. leading</li></ul>	<ul><li>Comfort zone</li><li>It's easier</li><li>I like doing it</li></ul>

After the coach and coachee have completed the Pain/Pleasure analysis, the coach simply has the coachee look at the completed form and asks, "What stands out to you?" Usually the coachee will do one of two things: either they will go to the biggest block or they will say something along the lines of, "I know what I need to do." If the coachee goes to the biggest block, then the coach simply returns to the Coaching Conversation model and tries to aid the coachee in problem-solving the block. If the coachee has the revelation of the best decision, then the coach returns to the Coaching Conversation model and helps the coachee build a plan of action.

Overall, the Pain/Pleasure analysis is highly effective in the decision-making process and helping coachees get "unstuck" and move to action. Once you help the coachee solve the blocks (as much as possible) and build out the motivators, then a simple comparison of the remaining blocks and motivators will likely reveal the best decision.

This analysis will NOT manipulate someone to a decision that is not right for them. The Pain/Pleasure analysis, in writing, simply speeds up the decision-making process. On a side note, it also reveals which topics a coachee is unlikely to change. For example, if the coachee can only verbalize the pain of delegating and the pleasure of not delegating and cannot generate any pain of not delegating or pleasure of delegating, then they are highly unlikely to shift their behavior.

Practice/Exercise

It can be helpful to first practice the Pain/Pleasure analysis on yourself. Think about a current decision that you need to make or some goal about which you have mixed feelings. Try to generate as many blocks and motivators as you can so that you fill in all four quadrants. Afterwards, ask yourself, "What stands out to me?" Then either work on solving your blocks or on building your action plan. After you have completed this analysis for yourself, practice on another person who will allow you to be a little "messy" as you master the process.

Pain/Pleasure Analysis

	Pain	Pleasure
Option #1		
Option #2		

Application

The Pain/Pleasure analysis is a highly impactful tool to help coachees who are stuck make decisions and move to action. The longer coachees stay in indecision, the more they drain themselves and miss opportunities. Use the Pain/Pleasure analysis to help coachees build confidence, make efficient decisions and take control over their lives. For more help in building confidence, refer to Dr. Ursiny's *The Confidence Plan*.

Quote

"May your choices reflect your hopes, not your fears."

— Nelson Mandela

Chapter 8: Being Fully Present and Connected

<u>**Story**</u>

We have made it a rule in our home that NO devices are allowed at our dinner table. Dinner time is just time for us to listen to one another, ask questions and be curious about each person's day. Being able to communicate and observe each other is needed in order to have an in-depth conversation. I think back on when I was a kid, and dinner as a family was a must and was a time for us to connect and catch up as a family. We would share what we learned, liked, and disliked and were asked questions by fellow family members. The good news was we not only learned from one another, we enjoyed conversing and looked forward to this time as a family each and every day.

With technology playing such a key role in our lives today, many parents like me are constantly coming up with rules about when or how our kids can earn "screen-time"; where they have it, how loud the headphones are set, and monitoring what is actually playing on those devices. We recognize that some screen time is good, but we know that the more time spent on our devices, the less time we focus on connecting with each other in a deep and meaningful way.

Coaches need to be fully present when working with their coachees. If we are coaching over the phone, we can't be multitasking and checking our email. Being fully present means listening, tracking with, observing (with all of our senses) and staying connected to the coachee. This requires discipline, focus and maintaining our own balance.

Overview

In this chapter, we'll cover some key coaching skills and tools that will help you raise your coaching expertise and increase your ability to stay fully present and connected. The five key skills we will review are: listening, the power of observation, intuition, self-management and metacommunication.

Listening

Listening is one of the hardest key coaching skills to master, yet we cannot overemphasize the importance of this foundational skill. A recent study pointed out that many of us spend between 70% and 80% of our day engaged in some form of communication, and about 55% of that time is devoted to **listening**. Some people are chattier than others, but on average the typical person utters anywhere from 125 to 175 words per minute. We find that a great coach will listen the vast majority of the time in a coaching conversation. The coachee should be doing the majority of the talking. Remember that in coaching, we are building a better problem-solver, not solving challenges for our coachees. If a coach is talking more than listening, they have likely stepped out of a pure coaching approach and are solving the coachee's problem for them. That is a fine approach when the primary goal is to solve the problem quickly, but not the best approach when you are trying to develop the other person.

The Coaching Conversation

There are three listening modes that we use in our coaching. As a coach we need to master all three and adapt to the coachee's specific listening need. See the differences below:

Three Listening Intentions

Intent	Purpose
Gather	Listen for information so that you fully understand the thoughts, issues, circumstances, etc., related to the topic at hand.
Empathize	Listen for emotions. How does the coachee feel about the topic?
Solve	Listen for clues in order to help the coachee self-discover potential solutions to the problem.

How do we become better listeners? Listening is abstract and it can be difficult to improve abstract skills unless we can make it more concrete. Therefore, we have found that the best way to improve your listening skills is to practice your reflection skills. By reflecting back information, emotions or potential solutions you hear the coachee verbalizing, you will be able to assess your mastery of each of these listening modes.

That said, as a coach, you are listening for several things beyond just the words and feelings expressed by the coachee. You are listening for:

- Assumptions that the coachee is making about themselves, others, or the situation

- Previous strategies used by the coachee

- Blocked thinking the coachee might have about the situation

- Patterns the coachee shows in handling challenges

- Hope and excitement expressed which can often create a path for solutions

- Competing goals or motivations felt by the coachee about the situation

- The impact of other relationships involved in the challenge or opportunity

- Strengths that might aid the coachee to take appropriate action

- Reactions they have to you

- Tentative language (try to, maybe, sort of, etc.) that may indicate a lack of total commitment to the process or solution

Picking up on these messages can help you determine the next set of questions that will help deepen your coachee's thinking process.

The Coaching Conversation

Power of Observation

Beyond words, we are also listening for and paying attention to such things as:

Voice or tone

So much is expressed by tone. Tone reveals a deeper emotion behind the topic being discussed. Say this sentence six times, but each time put the emphasis on the underlined word, noting how it changes the meaning of the sentence:

1. "<u>I</u> never said that you are a bad manager."

2. "I <u>never</u> said that you are a bad manager.

3. "I never <u>said</u> that you are a bad manager."

4. "I never said that <u>you</u> are a bad manager."

5. "I never said that you are a <u>bad</u> manager."

6. "I never said that you are a bad <u>manager</u>."

Note how each emphasis changes the meaning of the statement. The first suggests that "I" didn't say it, but someone else did. The second sounds defensive or adamant. Our third version sounds like we think it, but we haven't said it. The fourth intonation means, "I said it about someone else." The fifth version might suggest that the person is a mediocre manager, but not terrible. The final version hints that the person might be a fine manager, but they are bad at something else. This is one sentence! The words are identical, but by changing the tone we completely change the message.

So coaches listen astutely for tonality and hold a mirror up to the coachee to explore their tone. For example, if someone were to say, "I'm really excited about this opportunity," but shows zero excitement in their tone, the coach might reflect back, "I hear you say that you are excited about this and yet your voice doesn't sound very excited. So I'm curious about what's up?" This gives the coachee a chance to reflect on the veracity of their statement and clarify it to the coach and often to themselves. Now, note that the coach's tone is important here also. The most common tone in a coach's voice should be a tone of curiosity and definitely not a tone of judgment. Do the above reflection in a curious tone and then do it in an aggressive and judgmental tone. The difference is huge! When the content of the message and the tone are inconsistent, it is very likely the more accurate message lies in the tone. We like to say, "tone reveals truth." So, skilled coaches listen very intentionally for tonality.

Body language

If you meet with your coachees in person, you have an added advantage of reading their body language. That said, body language can often be misinterpreted and can represent different messages across cultures, so we are very careful in our interpretation of body language. Again, as a coach, it is not your job to judge the body language, but rather to observe it and when important, bring it up to the coachee. I remember once facilitating a group discussion and almost everyone in the room had their arms crossed. My first thought was, "What did I say that has gotten everyone so upset and defensive?" However, I knew better than to just go with that first impression, so I said to the group,

"Hey, I'm noticing a lot of crossed arms in the room, what's going on? (said in a curious tone)". They responded almost in unison, saying, "It is really cold in here!" What a mistake it would have been for me to verbalize something like, "Wow, looks like I really hit a nerve here; what did I say to make you all so defensive?" So observe body language, but be careful in your assumptions about its meaning.

Phone coaching, of course, does not allow you to observe body language. Therefore, non-visual indicators become even more important. The coach must pay even more attention to tonality, as well as things like language, volume, pacing, pauses, and sighs. Again, with these non-visual cues we need to be careful about over-interpreting. We also need to be willing to investigate these cues when they occur, asking things like, "I notice there is silence over the phone; what's up?"

Environment

Reading our coachee's environment can also help us pick up on clues as to their state of mind. If they are calling from their office, they may respond differently than if they were calling from home or in their car. Sometimes we hear the clacking of keyboard keys while we are coaching someone. Now, they might be taking notes on the session or they might be multitasking during the coaching call. So again, we simply reflect it back to them and let them clarify and decide. In general, when you are doing phone coaching, it is good to encourage your coachees to find a focused place from which they can call you that is free from distractions and interruptions.

As you can imagine, while these are three factors impacting the coach's observations of the coachee, they are also the same factors impacting the coachee's observation of the coach. Make sure your voice and body language reflect your preparedness for the call. This is especially true of your environment. If coachees can hear distractions in the background, they too are going to feel distracted. No multitasking, coaches!

Intuition

Another key coaching skill is the ability to utilize your intuition. When we express an intuition or a "hunch", we must remember that we are working with a perception rather than objective reality. A coach must be careful not to express an intuition as a fact or in a judging manner. However, a coach must also learn to trust his or her intuition as an indication of something occurring in the coaching relationship. Holding back on your intuitive thoughts can rob your coachee of valuable feedback or insights. The most important factor in expressing intuition is in your style of sharing the hunch. Below are some ways of sharing intuition that can either harm or aid the relationship.

Statements that can be harmful when sharing an intuitive sense:

- "I know exactly what you are experiencing and it is . . . . . "
- "There is something that you don't see about yourself here . . ."
- "It is obvious to me that you . . ."
- "I can see that the real issue is . . ."

These all share an arrogance where the coach is elevating him or herself above the coachee and they are unlikely to be received well. They also could potentially harm the relationship. Obviously we don't suggest using any of these.

Some statements that are much better for sharing intuition would be the following:

- "I may be completely off the mark with this, but let me share with you what I am thinking…"

- "See how this works for you …"

- "I wonder if…"

- "So, I am getting an instinctive feel that…"

- "I am not sure why I am thinking this, so I would like to check it out with you…"

With these examples, the coach is not assuming or making any judgments. These show more humility and a gentleness in sharing the instinctual feeling. They allow the coachee to reflect and make the decision. Paradoxically, by giving the coachee permission to say that you are wrong, they are actually more likely to say that you may be right.

Self-Management

Self-Management is the fourth skill associated with being a great coach and it is critical to mastering the other skills. This is an area of focus we must never neglect, as self-management helps us regulate our emotions and behaviors, thus leading to more patience, discernment and focus when working with our coachees. In this section we will discuss three ways to manage ourselves well.

The first is to show good self-care. Maintaining balance professionally and personally allows you to focus on coachee needs. When our life is out of balance, we are less likely to show good self-management, which can negatively impact our coaching. For example, if you are ill, it's better to reschedule your coaching calls instead of muddling through them and providing your coachees with mediocre coaching sessions. Whenever we are too sick, too tired or too stressed, our coachee is unlikely to receive our best abilities.

When we provide workshops for coachees on stress management, we usually do an exercise having them share their best stress-busting or recharging activities. Here is a partial list of some of the most common approaches our coachees have shared with us.

- Sleep
- Listen to calming or uplifting music
- Garden
- Pray
- Call a friend
- Do yoga or meditation
- Have a glass of wine
- Exercise

- Watch a comedy

- Get out into nature

- Write a venting letter

For coaches, it is not a luxury to take care of themselves; it is a responsibility. Perhaps you are what we call a Soft Soul (or have a coachee who is). Dr. Ursiny's book, *Soft Souls Living in a Harsh World* addresses how different types of soft souls can recharge and connect in their own way, with authenticity. This can then be used as another tool in your coach's toolbox with clients who happen to be soft souls.

The second self-management strategy is to know your hot buttons; identify human tendencies and behaviors that may irritate you during a coaching session. What tends to get you upset? What personality types challenge you most? How aware are you of your sensitive areas? Maybe laziness or arrogance or indecisiveness bothers you. Knowing yourself well, in advance, will help prevent the judging of your coachees, which is critical because few people will trust you if they feel judged by you. We will do an exercise at the end of this chapter to help you identify your main pet peeves in human behavior. Once you know your pet peeves it will help control your reaction. For example, if fearful behaviors irritate you and your coachee shows fear in completing his or her action steps, the unaware coach will show irritation and judgement, while the aware coach can control those reactions and patiently help their coachee address the feared actions.

The Coaching Conversation

The third self-management approach is to set up an advance strategy. We are all human and imperfect so there will be times when we are "triggered" in a coaching session. Therefore, it is critical to have strategies in place to handle these moments. For example, there may be occasions where a coachee gets irritated with you. Maybe you are encouraging them to stretch themselves or they don't like what was revealed in the coaching session. What are you going to do to handle that moment? What strategies will you have in place to deal with their anger toward you? Without an advance strategy, you may fall into a reactive stance or become defensive or passive. Having a strategy in place in advance will help you navigate the situation more skillfully. One of my strategies for dealing with anger is related to what we discussed in a previous chapter: I try to uncover the emotion behind the anger. It is much easier for me to deal with emotions like disappointment or hurt vs. dealing with someone venting anger at me. Another strategy I have (and this may sound silly to some of you) is to just have a mantra in my head of, "They have the right to express what they feel, just love them through this." This simple mantra helps me keep the focus on helping them vs. focusing on my own feelings or reactions. Other examples of situations that might require an advance strategy:

- Coachees who show a pattern of going over their allotted time
- Coachees who complain that the last session was not worth their time or money
- Someone you are coaching who is dealing with a challenge that is also an issue for you
- Late cancellations

- The coachee comes to the session completely unprepared

Advance strategies are most important to have around your areas of sensitivity or irritation in order to stay calm and focused on helping your coachee.

Metacommunication:

Returning to our list of the top skills that coaches should master leads us to metacommunication. Metacommunication is talking about how we are communicating. It is about stepping out of the details of the coaching conversation and talking about the dynamics of the communication. Sometimes communication between the coach and the coachee isn't working. If you feel off track, you will need to connect with your coachee to get the two of you aligned. Here are some examples you may experience and/or use:

- If you are confused about what is happening in the conversation you could ask, "What do you think is going on in our communication right now?"

- If you have let your mind wander, you could say, "I am sorry; I was letting my attention go elsewhere. I really want to focus on what we are dealing with. Could we get back to your main point in this discussion?"

- If there is tension in the conversation, you might say (with a nonjudgmental tone), "I'm noticing tension in this conversation; what can we shift to make it better?"

- If the coachee is scattered over a bunch of topics, you could say, "We are covering a lot of topics, where would you like to focus?"

- If the coachee is talking about something irrelevant to their coaching goals, you could refocus them by saying, "I am wondering what you want to accomplish from this discussion."

Some additional examples include:

- "As we are talking, I'm finding myself wondering how I can best aid you right now."

- "How are you feeling about the way our coaching is going?"

- "What do you think is the most important idea that you have shared?"

Metacommunication gives you and the coachee the opportunity to fix or realign the dynamics and focus on the conversation so that each coaching meeting can be productive and lead to positive results.

Practice/Exercise

What types of individuals irritate you the most? For example, I get very irritated on planes when the flight attendant says, "We have a full flight, so please do not put your second bag or your coats in the overhead compartment," and you see people throwing their bags and coats in the overhead. That irritates me! I see that as rude behavior. So, rude people bother me the most. Who bothers you the most? It could be any type of person, but you only get to choose 1 – 3 types. Some examples include the following:

- Lazy people

- Rude people

- Arrogant people

- Those who are always late

- Indecisive people

- Aloof individuals

- Cowards

Go ahead and write down 1 – 3 types of people who irritate you the most (do not read on until you have done this):

_____

_____

_____

Now, think about the opposite of what you wrote. For example, the opposite of "rude" would be "polite." The opposite of "aloof" would be something like "warm." Now, the opposite of the type of person who irritates you is likely an area of giftedness for you! I was raised by a single mother, so I am more polite than most men. If lazy people bother you, you probably have an incredible work ethic. If indecisive people bother you, you are probably a very decisive human being. We tend to judge people most harshly in our area of giftedness, and frankly that is wrong. You are the outlier! You are the weirdo (in a good way)! When we realize we are gifted in certain areas, it gives us more patience. Instead of judging the other person, we want to mentor and help them. And believe me, I have mentored a few guys on planes! Seriously! And as long as I take kind and loving energy to the conversation, it is often effective. It has never been effective when I have addressed them with irritation and judgment. People don't change when they feel judged. So use this insight to help you with your self-management.

Application

The techniques we have learned in this chapter are essential to being better communicators. As coaches, we are always striving to improve our craft and hone our skills. Here are a few questions you can ask yourself to help in this area:

- What else are you listening for aside from the words being spoken?

- How can you use your intuition to serve your coachee well in your relationship?

- Can you think of a recent miscommunication? How might you have used metacommunication to get the conversation back on track?

Quote

"The word 'listen' contains the same letters as the word 'silent'."

— *Alfred Brendel*

Section III: Tools and Perspectives for Coaching Common Challenges

Chapter 9: Employee Engagement and Career Satisfaction

<u>Story</u>

Greg was in charge of multiple branches for a large financial services firm and had been coaching with me for about four months. He called about ten minutes late for his coaching appointment and sounded exasperated. He expressed frustration with his team members for their negativity and talked about how they were actively resisting changes that he was in charge of implementing in the branches. Greg knew that many of the changes were unpopular, but also knew that he had to get his group aligned to these new processes, approaches and shifts. When asked about the changes, he shared that there were many, including layoffs, new technology, merging of branches, and changes in roles and responsibilities. This particular firm had gone through multiple changes in the last several years and people were feeling worn out, fearful and disengaged. "They keep complaining about things that I can't control and I am getting sick of it. How can I get them reengaged and cooperative?"

We first explored his current tactics for getting the group to a more positive space. "What do you do currently when the team expresses skepticism about the changes?" I asked. As we talked further, it was apparent that Greg was using very ineffective strategies. Some of the worst tactics to use with skeptics are to ignore their skepticism, argue with them about their skepticism, or try to over-sell them on the negative changes. Greg was doing all three of these to some degree. Once we determined that his previous tactics needed revamping and Greg was ready to try some new approaches, we brainstormed a possible approach to moving his team from skepticism to alignment. He implemented the following steps the next week.

Greg called the entire team together for a meeting to discuss all of the changes in the firm. As they entered the room, he handed everyone a pad of sticky notes and a marker and said that he wanted to understand all of the things that were frustrating the team currently (the sticky notes represent a technique called "storyboarding" that we will explain in more detail in our Achieving Results, chapter 10). Once everyone got situated, he asked the group, "So what is frustrating you at work right now?" As individuals yelled out a frustration he reflected it back to them (summarizing what they said), asked them to write it on the sticky note and put it on the wall and then said, "Absolutely. Good. What else?" Then he kept repeating this process until they had nothing else to add.

By the time Greg finished, he had over 30 sticky notes on the wall. He could tell immediately that the group felt a little better because instead of debating them or selling them, he had listened to them. But his job was not done yet. After reviewing the items on the notes he told the group that they were going to cluster the notes into three categories. Greg said, "The first category is things upon which you and I can have zero impact; they are absolutely out of our control and we can do nothing about them." After grouping those sticky notes together, he then asked them to pick from the remaining notes those things that only he could impact, things they had no ability to impact whatsoever. In the final cluster were things that everyone in the room could impact.

After forming these categories, Greg asked the group, "Now, what is it going to do to us if we spend all of our time focused on the items upon which we have zero impact?" One person shouted out, "We'll be miserable!" Another said, "It is a complete waste of our time!" Greg agreed and said, "O.K., for the sake of our sanity, from now on when one of these pops up in discussion, let's acknowledge it as real and then turn our focus to one of the other categories." The group showed their agreement. He went on to say, "And I am going to come back to you all in two weeks with some ideas on the things that are in the category of items that only I can impact." Greg continued, saying, "In that meeting I also want all of you to pick one or two things from the category of items that all of us can impact and come to that meeting with your plan for how you are going to make that impact." Because they felt heard and Greg modeled ownership, everyone agreed, came back in two weeks with their ideas and were now engaged and working together to solve the challenges.

Overview

The statistics around employee engagement are staggering. Gallup, Inc. has been sharing numbers for decades and we are seeing organizations try all kinds of solutions. Some focus on the environment by arranging fun and/or relaxing activities in the workplace. One organization we are familiar with had skating tracks in the office, basketball hoops, yoga rooms, nap rooms, wine and more. Other organizations are investing in coaching and professional development which focus on such things as organizational needs matched with employee interests and mentorship programs. Additionally, there are extensive evaluations available that look at employee engagement. These give leaders real time feedback from their teams with specific suggestions on improvement.

Below are the results of a 2017 Gallup, Inc. poll. Engagement is a big issue and has been for some time.

2017 Employee Engagement/Retention Statistics

- 85% of the global workforce is not engaged or actively disengaged (Gallup[6])

- Disengaged workers cause massive losses in productivity – between $450 and $500 billion a year (Harvard Business Review[7])

- It can cost 33% of an employee's salary to replace him/her (HR Dive[8])

- 75% of the causes of employee turnover are preventable (HR Dive[9])

Let's discuss the role coaching plays in employee engagement. If we go back to our early chapters on listening and opened-ended questions, we are reminded that the whole premise behind coaching is to allow the coachee to play the leading role in their show (their professional

---

[6] Jim Harter, "Dismal Employee Engagement Is a Sign of Global Mismanagement," https://www.gallup.com/workplace/231668/dismal-employee-engagement-sign-global-mismanagement.aspx

[7] Emma Seppälä and Kim Cameron, "Proof That Positive Work Cultures Are More Productive," https://hbr.org/2015/12/proof-that-positive-work-cultures-are-more-productive

[8] Valerie Bolden-Barrett, "Study: Turnover Costs Employers $15,000 per worker," https://www.hrdive.com/news/study-turnover-costs-employers-15000-per-worker/449142/

[9] Bolden-Barrett, "Study: Turnover Costs Employers $15,000 per worker"

life). What this means is even with designated job descriptions and role responsibilities, by design, coaching gives individuals an opportunity to shape and improve their roles and thus their engagement. Coaching supports this development by first understanding who they are as an individual, what their strengths are and how their present life fits into their role and future vision. The individualized nature of coaching immediately personalizes goal setting and professional development. It takes the whole person into account, whereas general employee standard operating procedures and guidelines simply cannot. We understand these structures are required for organizations to run efficiently, but coaching takes it a step further to engage an individual in a way that works for them.

By using coaching skills to listen to wants and unique ways of problem solving, coachees become involved in a way that has not been part of traditional management. In many cases, this approach requires a culture change within an organization. In this chapter we are reinforcing the value of the coaching skills and applying them to four primary employee engagement areas. When these areas are addressed, we see a turnaround in our disengaged coachees.

Effectively Communicate

Too often, communication is one way. In our story above, Greg had actually done a great job communicating all of the firm's changes to his team. He was open and transparent and modeled good informational communication. However, Greg was more challenged in letting his team communicate with him. He would ignore their concerns, debate their skepticism and would quickly move to talking about how great the changes would be in the long-term. This resulted in negative employees who felt like their leader was out of touch with their world and unconcerned with their losses and fears. Greg was trying to lead his team somewhere without taking the time to listen to them and validate their concerns. He was so worried about the team getting negative that he failed to let them vent. Now, that said, we have seen other leaders fail by listening but never leading their teams to a more positive viewpoint. After listening, Greg led them to take ownership for the morale of the office and empowered them to change the culture. The coaching process is truly a joint effort to achieve engagement.

Focus on Strengths

A focus on strengths is a natural motivator and increases confidence. This does not mean we do not look for areas of growth and development. Quite the contrary, coaching is often about addressing areas of improvement. Leading with strengths aids this process and keeps coachees moving in a successful direction. Holding strengths in the forefront creates a safer place for exploring the challenges. This requires a sincere belief that your coachee is capable, creative and whole. This can be difficult for some coaches. Advice often feels easier than allowing someone the time and space to think about what they really want and how they may go about it. In coaching we don't always know what is going on behind the scenes and what may be most impactful and productive at that time. Trust in your coachees' opinions and hear them out. Remember that they are more invested in a solution if they helped create it. Show confidence in their strengths and encourage them to apply their strengths to their position in the company.

When an employee's strengths are aligned with their function, they are much more likely to be engaged.

Promote a Culture of Positive Accountability

Open communication and focusing on strengths will build the foundation for engaging individuals with positive accountability. A punitive approach to accountability leaves individuals feeling drained and resentful even if results are accomplished. With open communication and guidance, coachees will build an accountability structure that supports them in succeeding. They will feel empowered and driven to reach their potential. When incorporating action items and follow-up in coaching, ask your coachees what type of structure would keep them most engaged. Feeling part of a larger effort encourages engagement. Practicing these concepts inside and outside of coaching sessions will contribute to creating a new culture.

Help Coachees Match Their Passions to Their Positions

While focusing on strengths is quite helpful for engagement and career satisfaction, just because we are skilled at something doesn't necessarily mean we are passionate about doing it for a living. Sometimes it is about the fit between a person's passions and position. When someone is discontent with their job, they often take assessments that will help them discover which specific careers might fit their interests. While we have encouraged our coachees to take these assessments at times, we have developed an alternative approach that helps create a template of passions and interests that can be applied when considering a specific career, or to explore the match of a current job to career passions.

The Coaching Conversation

We have coached using this tool hundreds of times and the results are different, unique and eye-opening every time. The tool is called the "Career Projection Exercise," or CPE for short, and it is used to help the coachee determine what they can do in their current position to make it more fulfilling, or to discover when it may be time to look for a different career.

Coaches can use the Career Projection Exercise (CPE) to help their coachees determine what they want in a career. We present the tool here, followed by instructions.

	1	2	3	4	5	6	7	8	9	10
Your Name	X	X	X							
Person #1	X			X	X				X	
Person #2		X		X		X				X
Person #3				X	X		X			
Person #4							X	X	X	
Person #5			X				X			X
What is Different?										
What is Similar?										

The Coaching Conversation

1. Have the coachee write their name in the space indicated.

2. Have them write the names of 5 people for whom they know something about their careers.

3. Notice that in each of the 10 numbered columns, there are 2 "X" markings, designating 2 of the people listed in the far left column.

4. For the 2 people indicated in each column, have your coachee compare their professions:

   - Look for differences/similarities in career duties and functions. For example:

     o For column 1, a difference might be that your coachee has a job that requires being around people, while person #1 sits in a cubicle and works by him or herself. A similarity might be that they both work for small companies.

     o For column 2, a difference might be that person #2 has a job that involves selling a product, while your coachee sells a service. A similarity might be that you both manage people.

     o Encourage the coachee to find one difference and one similarity for each of the career pairings.

5. Write the differences/similarities in the spaces provided.

6. Each column should have unique job characteristics. This exercise will work best if they do not repeat characteristics.

7. After completing all of these, have the coachee circle the quality or function in each column that is most interesting or fulfilling to them.

8. When you have finished, have them prioritize those they have selected in terms of the qualities most important to them for career satisfaction, and write them down in priority order. Add any qualities in a job that did not come through the CPE, but which they know are important to them.

What you have created with your coachee is a unique and personalized template they can apply to their current career or to other potential careers to help determine how fulfilled they will be. For example, we have worked with many people who have been completely miserable in their current position. Often, the CPE reveals that one or more of their top career passions are completely missing from their current position. This is usually quite eye-opening for our coachees. We also use the CPE for our coachees who are job hunting. After completing it, we help them build a list of questions to ask potential employers to determine how well the job will fit. In addition, if a coachee is in a job that they prefer to keep, but many elements of the CPE are not being met they can work with their coach to determine how some of these passions could be satisfied through things like volunteer work or hobbies.

If you found someone else who knows the same five people, the CPE would end up with a completely different result. This exercise causes the coachee to project onto those roles the things they care about, passions they have, and different perspectives. We have never had two people create the same results on the CPE.

So, while the Career Projection Exercise will not tell you that you should be a lawyer or doctor or anything else, it does result in a personal, unique and solid template to help you gain insights into your current position or possible future careers.

Practice/Exercises

Exercise #1: Do the CPE on yourself. What insights does it give you into your own career passions? How well does your current position match your career passion priorities? How well do your passions fit with being a coach?

Exercise #2: Do the CPE on a friend or coachee who would like insights into their career path. Make sure that you are patient with the process. The exercise can be a struggle and a little tedious for some, but the outcome is worth it!

Application

If your coachee is struggling with engagement or career satisfaction (or leading others in these areas), consider all of the elements of this chapter and determine your best approach to coaching them to success.

Quote

"Employee engagement is the emotional commitment the employee has to the organization and its goals."

– Kevin Kruse [Employee Engagement 2.0]

Chapter 10: Achieving Results

Story

If there is anyone who has been successful at adapting to change, creating new goals and setting an example, it is Peyton Manning. If you do not know his history here is a synopsis:

- He started his career as a quarterback for the Indianapolis Colts, who, up to that point, had a long losing streak.

- He stayed with the Colts for 13 years and that is 3 times longer than the average NFL career.

- By his 13th year he had major neck injuries, and everyone assumed his career was over.

- Even with these injuries he was willing to do what was necessary to continue to play and lead his team.

- In his 14th year as quarterback with the Colts he was traded to the Denver Broncos.

With the change of environment, Peyton had to set new goals for himself. His confidence was a bit shaken when he was traded and he had the added pressure of a contract that stated that his neck needed to be a non-issue for at least 3 of the 5 years. Given his tenacity and focus, the move was a success. He went on to lead the Denver Broncos to the Super Bowl in 2014 and again in 2016 when they won the title.

Overview

What makes the Peyton Manning story so inspiring is the fact that he had to overcome several obstacles, both internal and external, in order to achieve his goals. Our role as coaches is to help our coachees identify those blocks and find ways to move past them in order to accomplish goals in life and work. In this chapter we will present two tools that we use in our own coaching practices to help coachees identify where they are getting stuck and help them remove their blocks. They are Storyboarding and the Blocks List.

The technique of storyboarding has been credited to animator Webb Smith who worked for the Walt Disney Company. Webb drew scenes on separate pieces of paper and then pinned them up on a bulletin board to create the sequence of the scene. Since then, storyboarding has often been used in film creation, but has also been adapted for use as a business and life brainstorming strategy.

Storyboarding can help coachees unblock their thinking, clear out their thoughts and take a concept from brainstorming to creating an action plan. The technique can be used for multiple tasks, including:

- Creating a marketing plan
- Clarifying roles and responsibilities on a team
- Planning a physical move between locations
- Prioritizing goals for coaching

- Creating a vision for your life or business

- Creating a presentation

- Planning an event

- Creating a to-do list

- Writing a book

Storyboarding can be used anytime you have a multifaceted challenge with many different pieces that you want to take from the idea stage to goal achievement.

In this method, the coachee writes down everything on their mind on separate sticky notes. Once they have flushed out all of their thoughts, the coach asks them to cluster the separate notes by categories. Once the categories are created, the coachee can prioritize the goals and create the needed action steps to move the goals forward.

Let's use the example of storyboarding to brainstorm and prioritize your career goals. You would use the following steps:

1. Brainstorm all of the career goals you have or tasks you need to complete right now to reach those goals.

2. Put each goal or task on a sticky note.

3. Cluster goals and tasks that appear to be related. Label the categories.

4. Determine if anything needs to be added to any of the categories.

5. Prioritize your categories.

6. Prioritize the goals and tasks within the categories.

7. For your top priority categories, break each goal or task into Specific, Measurable, Actionable, Realistic, and Timed (SMART) goals.

8. Record these goals and review them on a regular basis.

Again, this is just one example of using this technique. The uses of storyboarding are only limited by your imagination and you can use it in multiple situations. Remember our story about Greg from the previous chapter? That was an example of using storyboarding to accomplish the goal of getting a team out of negativity and focused on things they can control.

For more information on storyboarding, refer to Dr. Ursiny's and Carole Cowperthwaite-O'Hagan's book, *Tough Times Tactics*.

Another simplistic tool that we use in coaching is the Blocks List. The Blocks List is a direct way to help organize and jumpstart the coaching conversation. It is most appropriate for coachees who are highly self-aware and can be used as early as the first coaching session. We utilize this tool when we have a coachee who knows what they want but feels blocked or stuck on the way to achieve the desired goal, or they simply want to work on anything that could keep them at a lower level of performance. We introduce the tool as a list of the most common blocks individuals experience and ask the coachee to self-assess their challenges. The tool looks like this:

The Coaching Conversation

The Blocks to Optimal Performance List

Rate the following on a scale of 1-7 in terms of how much you struggle with each of them.

(7 = struggle constantly with this block; 1 = never struggle in this area.)

_____ Fear of failure   _____ Fear of success

_____ Procrastination   _____ Perfectionism

_____ Negative self-image   _____ Poor time management skills

_____ Lack of assertiveness   _____ Poor organizational skills

_____ Difficulty balancing work and home   _____ Lack of self-confidence

_____ Poor communication skills _____ Stagnation in comfort zones

_____ Anger/frustration   _____ Negative habits

_____ Lack of fulfillment at work   _____ Low self-discipline

_____ Inadequate goal setting   _____ Difficulty giving feedback to others

_____ Dealing poorly with conflict   _____ Poor listening skills

_____ Other (describe): _____

Once this is filled out you ask the coachee to choose an area of challenge and then laser-focus on coaching them past this block. While simplistic, the tool does help direct the coaching session and can give the coach and coachee a list to return to if they experience challenges in achieving a coaching goal.

Practice/Exercises

Exercise #1: Practice storyboarding

Choose an area in your own life to storyboard. Your choice could be anything that has multiple angles or ideas to it. You can pick anything from building a marketing plan for your coaching business to creating your vision for your career next year. I even had a corporate client practice this tool using his plans for building his family's in-ground pool. Follow the steps described below to create an action plan.

1. Brainstorm all the challenges, tasks or elements of your chosen area.

2. Put each idea on a sticky note.

3. Once your ideas are exhausted, cluster things that appear to be related.

4. Label the clustered categories.

5. Determine if anything needs to be added to any of the categories.

6. Prioritize your categories.

7. Prioritize the ideas within the categories.

8. For your top priority categories, break each goal or task into Specific, Measurable, Actionable, Realistic, and Timed (SMART) goals.

9. Record these goals and review them on a regular basis.

How was your experience with storyboarding?

The Coaching Conversation

In what areas might you use this tool with your coachees?

Exercise #2: Fill out the Blocks List for yourself.

The Blocks to Optimal Performance List

Rate the following on a scale of 1-7 in terms of how much you struggle with each of them.

(7 = struggle constantly with this block; 1 = never struggle in this area).

_____ Fear of failure   _____ Fear of success

_____ Procrastination   _____ Perfectionism

_____ Negative self-image   _____ Poor time management skills

_____ Lack of assertiveness   _____ Poor organizational skills

_____ Difficulty balancing work and home   _____ Lack of self-confidence

_____ Poor communication skills   _____ Stagnation in comfort zones

_____ Anger/frustration   _____ Negative habits

_____ Lack of fulfillment at work   _____ Low self-discipline

_____ Inadequate goal setting   _____ Difficulty giving feedback to others

_____ Dealing poorly with conflict   _____ Poor listening skills

_____ Other (describe): _____

What stands out to you?

How might you improve in these areas?

Exercise #3: Try storyboarding with a friend or coachee.

Exercise #4: If appropriate, have a coachee fill out the Blocks List and use it to focus your coaching sessions.

Application

Storyboarding and the Blocks List are tools to help coachees organize their thoughts and goals and get past blocks to achieving what they want in life and work. Sit down with a list of coachees with whom you are working. With which coachees might you use each of these tools? Specifically think about coachees who are struggling with complex goals (for storyboarding) and coachees who seem stuck, but have enough self-awareness to rate themselves realistically (for the Blocks List).

Many coachees we have worked with were most interested in increasing sales and/or getting to the next level. Let's face it, most of us need to use at least a modicum of persuasion/sales techniques in our day-to-day lives, so why not figure out how best to do that? The focus of Dr. Ursiny's book *Coaching the Sale* is about just that.

Quote

"Setting goals is the first step in turning the invisible into the visible".

— Tony Robbins

Chapter 11: Emotions in the Workplace

<u>**Story**</u>

Michael is a coachee of mine and he has given me permission to share his story regarding emotions in the workplace and the impact of perceptions and adverse reactions. It was annual review time and Michael was to meet with his boss, Steve, for his review. He was feeling pretty good going into the meeting and was confident that it would go well. When Steve began, he methodically went over Michael's review, section by section. However, as he progressed, Michael became more and more uncomfortable and disappointed with what Steve was saying. In fact, it became so offensive he turned away and ignored the rest of what was said and decided to say nothing. Once Steve finished, he asked if Michael had any questions and again Michael said nothing. Steve asked him to sign the review, which is common practice, and Michael said he would not and stormed out of his office. Steve was confused and puzzled, as he thought he gave Michael a pretty good review. Michael, on the other hand, left frustrated and angry. Here we had two people perceiving one conversation quite differently.

Michael and I had a scheduled coaching call shortly after and his first few words were, "I just had the worst review of my entire professional career." I asked him some open-ended questions such as, "What happened?" and "How did this make you feel?" He was extremely upset and felt wronged by his "terrible review". My goal was to listen so that I completely understood the situation and yet I also wanted to dig deeper into Michael's perceptions and emotions concerning the interaction. Michael decided he would take on the action step of reconnecting with Steve after he cooled down. His goal was to be direct about his level of disappointment. As an accountability measure, he agreed to touch base again immediately after having the conversation with Steve. In order to make sure that he could approach the conversation calmly, I took him through a method we call TruthTalk to help him analyze his emotions and perceptions (we will walk through this process in detail later in the chapter). As Michael worked through this method, he self-discovered that he was saying things to himself about the review that were not true and were not helpful. He came up with more truthful and helpful thoughts and he calmed down. Michael realized that his review was overall a good one and not "terrible" as he stated earlier. He now felt prepared to have a more productive conversation with his boss.

Well, as you probably guessed, when Michael and I spoke again his demeanor and disposition had changed. He shared with me that Steve was shocked by his reaction and shared that he actually gave him a great review! From their discussion, Michael and Steve realized that there was really just one line item on the review on which they disagreed and that it was during the discussion of that item that Michael shut down. Now, with emotion out of the equation, they were able to have a very productive conversation about his area for improvement.

Often in the workplace we interpret an interaction quite differently than someone else. These perceptions lead to emotions, and negative emotions often overcome logic. This is especially true if it is a high-stress situation or there are high stakes for the outcome. To make matters more complicated, emotions can scare people off from problem solving or even coaching. The bottom line is that emotions are everywhere in the workplace and it's helpful to have a strategy for dealing with them. When emotions are based on healthy perceptions and strategies are put in place to work through them, uncomfortable situations can turn into opportunities for growth.

Overview

Rational-Emotive Behavior Therapy is a form of therapy that addresses and helps replace self-defeating thoughts that cause us to exaggerate danger and focus on things we can't control. Research[10] has shown that revealing and changing these beliefs can lead to greater success, emotional stability and happiness. TruthTalk© is based on this technique and focuses on the demotivating things we can say to ourselves in the workplace.

We form negative perceptions and beliefs that can impact our confidence and create a great deal of insecurity during difficult times. Some common beliefs that can hold you back from your best confident self are:

- I'm powerless

- Everything is bad and it is always going to be this way

- I am sure that more horrible news is coming

- Failure is awful

- I can't deal with this

- This review is terrible!

---

[10] Albert Ellis, Ph.D. and Robert A. Harper, Ph.D., *A Guide to Rational Living* (Wilshire Book Co., 1975)

The Coaching Conversation

These are not statements of fact. These are perceptions or beliefs that we form out of our own insecurities. These thoughts interfere with our focus and suck out the energy we need to maximize performance in difficult work conditions. Parallels to these thoughts that are more truthful and more conducive to high confidence are:

- There is always something I can impact even if it is just my attitude

- Most challenges also bring opportunities and it serves me better to look for those

- I am going to prepare for whatever the future holds

- Failure is part of life and I can learn from every mistake

- Through focus and tenacity, I can tackle the current challenges

- There were some things I didn't like about this review, but also some really good scores and positive comments

With a little practice you can eliminate negative or performance-reducing thoughts and replace them with a mindset and attitude that will take you to your next level of confidence. If you do a series of these exercises, you will start noticing patterns in what kinds of thoughts decrease your confidence. Once you see the patterns you have more power to change them. It may be helpful to refer to Dr. Ursiny's *The Top Performer's Guide to Attitude* for additional suggestions.

The TruthTalk© Thought Tracking System is used in coaching to empower the coachee to take control of his/her thoughts that may be causing emotional distress. We can use the story from above with Michael and Steve to walk through the exercise.

TruthTalk© Thought Tracking System

The Catalyst for your Reaction: What happened? (Just the facts)	Self-talk Response: What did you say to yourself about it?	Emotional Response: How did you feel at the time and afterwards?	Behavioral Response: What did you do in response to the event?	Truth Test: Is what you are saying to yourself 100% true?	Strategic Test: Are your responses helping you or hurting you?

We always start with the column on the far left. What was the catalyst for the emotional response? It's imperative in the first column to state the facts and facts only. For example, Michael could NOT put "I got a terrible review" in the first column. That is a perception, not a fact. When asked to describe the actual content of the review that upset him, he said that on a scale of 1 – 5 where "1" means low and "5" means mastery of the behavior, Steve gave him multiple ratings of "4". So what we put in the first column was "Steve gave multiple ratings of "4".

The Coaching Conversation

The Catalyst for your Reaction: What happened? (Just the facts)	Self-talk Response: What did you say to yourself about it?	Emotional Response: How did you feel at the time and afterwards?	Behavioral Response: What did you do in response to the event?	Truth Test: Is what you are saying to yourself 100% true?	Strategic Test: Are your responses helping you or hurting you?
Steve gave multiple ratings of "4"					

Before addressing the self-talk response, we jump to the third column in the process to ask

about feelings. Michael reported multiple emotions, including anger and disappointment.

The Catalyst for your Reaction: What happened? (Just the facts)	Self-talk Response: What did you say to yourself about it?	Emotional Response: How did you feel at the time and afterwards?	Behavioral Response: What did you do in response to the event?	Truth Test: Is what you are saying to yourself 100% true?	Strategic Test: Are your responses helping you or hurting you?
Steve gave multiple ratings of "4"		Angry and disappointed			

We then recorded Michael's behavioral response of refusing to sign the review and leaving

Steve's office.

The Catalyst for your Reaction: What happened? (Just the facts)	Self-talk Response: What did you say to yourself about it?	Emotional Response: How did you feel at the time and afterwards?	Behavioral Response: What did you do in response to the event?	Truth Test: Is what you are saying to yourself 100% true?	Strategic Test: Are your responses helping you or hurting you?
Steve gave multiple ratings of "4"		Angry and disappointed	Refused to sign the review and left Steve's office		

The main premise of TruthTalk© is that events cannot dictate our feelings. We know intuitively that this is true because two people could go through the same experience and feel very differently about it. So the review cannot dictate to Michael that he feels angry and disappointed; what Michael is saying to himself about the review is what creates his emotions and then his behavioral choices. So I asked Michael, "What are you saying to yourself about the review that is making you angry and disappointed and caused you to leave his office?" After multiple attempts he came up with two thoughts/perceptions that were making him feel that way.

The Coaching Conversation

- This is a terrible review

- Steve doesn't see all the value I bring

The Catalyst for your Reaction: What happened? (Just the facts)	Self-talk Response: What did you say to yourself about it?	Emotional Response: How did you feel at the time and afterwards?	Behavioral Response: What did you do in response to the event?	Truth Test: Is what you are saying to yourself 100% true?	Strategic Test: Are your responses helping you or hurting you?
Steve gave multiple ratings of "4"	This is a terrible review Steve doesn't see the value I bring	Angry and disappointed	Refused to sign the review and left Steve's office		

The final two columns are the "test" portion of the exercise. After the coachee has had an opportunity to walk through all the columns, there is often relief in being able to vent. The two test columns give coachees a chance to reflect on what is "true." For instance, is it 100% true that Steve does not see Michael's value or 100% true that the review was "terrible"? In the moment, Michael believed that. However, given the opportunity to reflect on it, he said that neither were 100% true. (Note that the coachee has to be the one to decide that, not the coach).   Even if the coachee believes their self-talk is 100% true, the second test keeps them from focusing on thoughts that are destructive in any form; that second test is the "strategic test". In this portion of TruthTalk©, you simply ask the coachee if their self-talk and their behavioral response are helping them or hurting them. Michael was highly aware that getting mad and leaving his boss' office was likely not helping him.

The Catalyst for your Reaction: What happened? (Just the facts)	Self-talk Response: What did you say to yourself about it?	Emotional Response: How did you feel at the time and afterwards?	Behavioral Response: What did you do in response to the event?	Truth Test: Is what you are saying to yourself 100% true?	Strategic Test: Are your responses helping you or hurting you?
Steve gave multiple ratings of "4"	This is a terrible review Steve doesn't see the value I bring	Angry and disappointed	Refuse to sign the review and left Steve's office	No	Hurting

If the thought is 100% true AND is helpful, then the coachee should be encouraged to keep the thought, but if it fails EITHER test then we work with the coachee to come up with a new thought to replace the one that is either not provable or is hurtful. In Michael's case he came up with the new thought of, "While I disagree with some things on the review, overall it was positive. I am going to go back and have a productive talk with Steve." This allowed him to go back calmly and work through the review in a positive fashion.

With TruthTalk$^{©}$, you are able to help the coachee self-discover the assumptions and perceptions that drive their emotions and behaviors. Taking a coachee through this process often leads to relief and a positive focus. During our coaching certification program, many coaches in training are excited to have a tool like this. It also generates more questions than some of the other tools. Some of the questions we receive most frequently are, "How do I know when it's the appropriate time to use this tool?" and "What do I say to a person who is in the middle of an upsetting story?" These are valid questions. It can be awkward to ask someone to do an exercise during an emotional time. The key is to listen first and make sure your coachee has had the chance to vent and be heard. Then, get permission to use the tool, using such coaching questions as, "It sounds like this is really upsetting to you. How open would you be to walking through an exercise that might help you with this?" Once you have agreement, using the tool becomes less awkward.

Practice/Exercises

Exercise #1: Simplified Procedure for Changing Self-Talk

1. Pick a current or past situation that is upsetting you more than you want it to. Use your "TruthTalk© Tracking Form" to analyze if what you are saying to yourself about the catalyst is true and is helping you.

2. If the thought is helping you, then keep it. If the thought is not helping you or isn't 100% true, then find a more positive (but truthful) thought to say to yourself.

3. Put the new "thought" on an index card.

4. Every single time you catch yourself saying the old thought, pull out your index card and read the new thought over and over.

The Catalyst for your Reaction: What happened? (Just the facts)	Self-talk Response: What did you say to yourself about it?	Emotional Response: How did you feel at the time and afterwards?	Behavioral Response: What did you do in response to the event?	Truth Test: Is what you are saying to yourself 100% true?	Strategic Test: Are your responses helping you or hurting you?

New thought:

_____

_____

_____

Exercise #2: Preemptive TruthTalk©

Another way to use this tool is preemptively.

1. Think about a situation coming up in which you may struggle with your emotions. This may be an upcoming review like our story earlier in this chapter or a tough conversation you may need to have with a colleague.

2. Write down self-statements that are true that will help you get through it. For example, if you are preparing for your performance evaluation you might write down in advance such self-statements as:

   - "I know that I have done a good job."

   - "I don't expect other people to be perfect so I won't expect that of myself."

   - "I will use this experience to learn about growth areas; it is about progress, not perfection."

   - "I will pay just as much attention to the positive things said as to the negative."

   - "I will assertively stand up to any evaluation that seems unfair without being defensive."

Preemptive thoughts:

_____

_____

_____

3. Practice these before the event.

Exercise #3: Practice with a coachee

Use the TruthTalk© Thought Tracking form with a coachee to help them self-discover the

connection between their thoughts, emotions and actions and help them take control of their

responses.

The Catalyst for your Reaction: What happened? (Just the facts)	Self-talk Response: What did you say to yourself about it?	Emotional Response: How did you feel at the time and afterwards?	Behavioral Response: What did you do in response to the event?	Truth Test: Is what you are saying to yourself 100% true?	Strategic Test Are your responses helping you or hurting you?

Application

TruthTalk$^{©}$ is applicable any time your coachee is having a strong and potentially harmful emotional reaction to an event. It is a methodical way to help your coachee examine their responses and take control of their emotions. Coaches must remember that they are always dealing with the coachee's perspectives and not necessarily reality. While it is not the coach's job to determine reality, TruthTalk$^{©}$ helps the coachee move from a highly emotional response to a more logical response. They examine and self-discover their perceptions and then make their own choice about how they will deal with the situation.

Quote

"A negative mind will always struggle to see and create a positive outcome."

— Ty Howard

Chapter 12: Time Management

Story

Many people struggle with time management, but I have one coachee named Dave who really sticks out from the crowd. Dave is a financial advisor and, like many people in a sales role, he is excellent with his clients but really struggles with his organizational skills. On our first call, Dave said that he wanted to get better at time management, saying, "I feel as if I am running like a hamster in a cage on one of those wheels going 'round and 'round and going nowhere. I work hard, but I know that I waste a ton of time and my work effort is not reflected in production. On top of that, I am exhausted each day and feel like a failure. I've tried lots of fancy time management systems, but nothing works with me."

We looked at what he wanted to achieve, examined what was getting done and identified his specific time management challenges, which were planning, procrastination and scheduling. Once we clarified his strengths and speedbumps, we focused first on the planning of his day. Since "fancy" time management systems intimidated him, we created baby steps by getting three things planned and done each day. We built this up slowly over time until he had implemented this as a new habit. We used the same baby step approach with his scheduling challenges and dealt with his procrastination tendencies using the Pain/Pleasure analysis discussed earlier in the book and also demonstrated later in this chapter.

By approaching his time management in a non-threatening step-by-step method, Dave was able to focus his dedication and drive and get better results. By achieving small wins along the way he was able to stay motivated and we built on each success to go to the next level. Dave stands out above some of my other coachees because he increased his productivity by **3-4 hours a day!**

Overview

Time management is a common challenge for many and there are plenty of systems out there to help people manage their time. In 20 years, we have seen some clear patterns when it comes to coachees wanting to manage their schedules to include productive work days while still having a life outside of the office. At Advantage Coaching and Training, the four most common areas we address to help with time mastery are planning, time tracking, overcoming procrastination and delegating well.

Planning

Planning is the most simplistic of the three areas, in that time blocking is often the most effective method for planning appropriately. When coaching on time blocking, there are several key elements, including:

- What should be the frequency of blocking time out for planning?

- If weekly, then what day of the week would be best?

- What time of day would be most effective for time blocking?

- How much time do they think is reasonable to commit to the planning process?

- What is the process they will follow during this time?

- How can they make sure they protect this time?

Once coachees find the value of time blocking and are held accountable for a period of time, this behavior often turns into a powerful habit.

Time tracking

Sometimes we have coachees who lack awareness as to the time-draining elements of their day. They leave the office wondering where their time went. Whenever we have a coachee who is baffled by their lack of time, we recommend using a time tracking form. The time tracking form typically consists of five columns that address:

1. Time increments – The actual time in the day (these can be divided into 15 or 30 minute segments).

2. Activity log – The coachee briefly records what they are doing during that time increment.

3. Highest and best use of time – They assess if that particular activity is the highest and best use of their talent.

4. Potential to delegate – To whom (if anyone) could this task be delegated?

5. Interruptions – They record the nature of anything or anyone that interrupts them.

The Coaching Conversation

Sample time tracking form:

Time increments	Activity log	Highest and best use of time (yes or no)?	To whom could you delegate this task?	Interruptions
9:00 – 9:30				
9:30 – 10:00				
10:00 – 10:30				
10:30 – 11:00				
11:00 – 11:30				
11:30 – 12:00				
12:00 – 12:30				
12:30 – 1:00				
1:00 – 1:30				
1:30 – 2:00				
2:00 – 2:30				
2:30 – 3:00				
3:00 – 3:30				
3:30 – 4:00				
4:00 – 4:30				
4:30 – 5:00				

The Coaching Conversation

When introduced to the idea of time tracking, our coachees often respond, "I don't have the time to do that!" While we never force our coachee to do anything, we do highly encourage them to experience the short-term pain of tracking their time in order to experience the long-term relief of being in control of their time.

Once they complete the time tracking for two weeks, we have them bring it to their coaching session. We explore together the insights discovered and help them build plans to delegate, put boundaries up against frequent interruptions, and cluster similar activities in order to increase their efficiency.

Overcoming procrastination:

Procrastination is another common enemy to effective time management. Procrastination can have many negative results, such as wasted mental energy, errors in doing things at the last minute, frustration to peers who are impacted by the procrastination, and guilt.

Usually when coaching on procrastination, we will use the Pain/Pleasure analysis from Chapter 7. This analysis will help us uncover their specific blocks and motivators to completing tasks in a better timeline. It also acts as a motivator for the coachee as they really see and feel the negative impact of procrastinating. Below is a Pain/Pleasure chart specifically designed to address procrastination.

	Pain	Pleasure
Continue procrastinating		
Do tasks sooner		

Once they complete this, the coach can zero in on specific blocks and help the coachee develop strategies for overcoming those blocks. The coach can also aid the coachee in strategically using their motivators to help change their behavior.

While the blocks and motivators are unique to the individual coachee, several best practices exist for breaking procrastination, including the following:

- Develop clear goals

- Break down challenges into doable steps

- Keep your goals constantly present

- Focus on your behavior as the goal, not the outcome

- Make it more painful NOT to do the goal and focus on the pleasure of eliminating the "mind traffic" and guilt

Delegating and/or setting priorities:

Delegating is the act of giving work over to someone else. The purpose is usually to grow and empower your people, to keep you in the highest and best use of your time and to create greater overall long-term results for the organization.

Again, we often use the Pain/Pleasure analysis to uncover blocks and motivators to delegating well. The most common blocks are the fear of the task not being done well, the fear of losing control and the time it takes to teach someone to do the task (coachees often say, "It is faster to do it myself."). The most common motivators to becoming a better delegator include, "I'm too busy and this will save time in the long-term", "I enjoy empowering and growing people" and "We will get better results long-term if I do this." Through coaching, coachees usually realize that the short-term time it takes to teach someone is worth the long-term time they save. To address the fears of losing control or the project going badly, we help coachees develop reporting structures that define both the amount of power the individual is being granted and the reporting structure for the project. Clarity in these two areas often allows the coachee to become a better delegator and decrease their fears. Let's explore the main steps to delegation and then also look at the options for empowerment and reporting.

There are five main steps to the delegation process.

Step 1: Analyze your mind - Many times our blocks to being effective delegators have to do with self-imposed issues. We uncover these by using the Pain/Pleasure analysis.

Step 2: Be purposeful in choosing to whom you delegate – Match the tasks, functions, and projects to your assessment of others' strengths and readiness. Several factors go into this decision, such as the risk level of the task, how much you trust the person, the individual's skill sets, their historical behaviors, their experience and the level of motivation they demonstrate toward the task.

Step 3: Decide level of empowerment and reporting structure

- Decision #1: Determine the ideal level of empowerment

    o Low – An example of low power would be having them collect information, run an analysis and share the data or results.

    o Medium – An example of medium power would be to have them analyze the project and come back with their recommendations. This helps you assess their level of judgment or discernment.

    o High – An example of high power would be to empower them to make the actual decision.

- Decision #2: Determine the level of monitoring/reporting

    o Full involvement – This should be used sparingly, as most people dislike being micromanaged and may assume you don't trust them. That said, if the project is highly important and the delegate has not had experience with the project, then you may need to check in often.

    o Frequent check-in – This is where you would have the delegate give written or verbal reporting at a defined frequency, such as every Monday at 10:00 AM.

    o Occasional check-in – For longer projects, the check-in times could be made less frequent, but still at a set day or time.

    o Reactive – They only need to check in if they have challenges or problems.

    o No monitoring – They completely own the project and do not need to check in at all with you (obviously this is only given after experience with the person where they have demonstrated great problem-solving skills and reliability).

Step 4: Communicate clearly – While it should go without saying, make sure the delegate knows their level of power and the reporting structure.

Step 5: Provide ongoing feedback and coaching – Unless the person was given full authority to make the decision with no need to report back, we would want to give them feedback and coaching to help them celebrate successes, learn from mistakes, and continue to grow in their abilities.

While simplistic, we have found that coaching your coachee through these five steps leads to effective delegation and the enjoyment of freeing up their time.

Practice/Exercises

Exercise #1: Time blocking

What is an important activity or task that you have not been addressing as much as you would like? Use time blocking to make an appointment with yourself each week to help increase your focus on this. Answer the following questions to get started.

1. What should be the frequency of blocking out the time?

2. If weekly, then what day of the week would be best?

3. What time of day would be most effective for this time blocking?

4. How much time is reasonable to commit to this activity or task?

5. What is the process you will follow during this time? What are you actually going to do?

6. How will you protect this time?

The Coaching Conversation

Exercise #2: Using the time tracking form

Try the time tracking form for one day. While we usually recommend two weeks, doing this form for a day will at least give you a sense of what you are asking your coachee to do. Fill in the time increments that are appropriate for your day.

Time increments	Activity log	Highest and best use of time (yes or no)?	To whom could you delegate this task?	Interruptions

The Coaching Conversation

Exercise #3: Coaching someone to overcome procrastination

If you are working with someone struggling with procrastination, then do a Pain/Pleasure analysis with them. Use the information that you gather to help them build a plan to overcome their blocks and focus on their motivators.

	Pain	Pleasure
Continue procrastinating		
Do tasks sooner		

Exercise #4: Examining delegation

What is something in your day that takes up your time, but is not the highest and best use of your time? Use the delegation steps to empower someone else to handle this activity or project.

Step 1: Analyze your mind – If you feel blocked or have concerns about delegating, then do a Pain/Pleasure analysis. If not, then go on to step 2.

Step 2: Be purposeful in choosing to whom you delegate – Who would be the best person for this task? Consider their skill sets, historical behaviors, experience and motivation level.

Step 3: Decide level of empowerment and reporting structure

- Decision #1: How much power do you want to give this individual: low, medium or high? Describe specifically what this level of power enables them to do.

  _____

  _____

  _____

- Decision #2: For this activity, what would be the appropriate level of monitoring/reporting? Describe the frequency below:

  _____

  _____

  _____

Step 4: Communicate clearly – Communicate the decisions you made above with the individual.

Step 5: Provide ongoing feedback and coaching – If appropriate, make sure you give both positive feedback and critique during your check-in times and coach them to success!

Application

Time management is a common topic for coaching and this chapter gives you four approaches to help coachees master their time. While some of the methods act as suggestions vs. the Socratic method, the coach is most effective when the approaches are simply guidelines and the coaching process is the true start of the interaction.

Quote

"Never leave 'til tomorrow what you can do today."

– Benjamin Franklin

Conclusion

Little did we know that a simple dinner in 1998 would lead to three people becoming long-term colleagues and lifelong friends. Over the last 20 years we have seen coaching grow and develop in substance and in popularity. We have had the wonderful privilege of training and certifying hundreds of coaches and also impacting the cultures of some Fortune 100 firms. The journey has been incredible.

This book represents many of the perspectives, approaches and tools we have used for decades to help people develop and achieve their goals. Whether you are an internal coach in an organization or an external coach running your own business, we sincerely hope that the content in this book will help enhance your skills and impact lives.

About the Authors

Timothy Ursiny, Ph.D., RCC™

Dr. Tim Ursiny, founder of Advantage Coaching & Training, Inc., is a speaker and certified business coach specializing in helping individuals reach peak performance and life satisfaction. He is a member of the International Coach Federation and the Worldwide Association of Business Coaches. His areas of expertise include communication skills, emotional intelligence, team building, leadership, coaching skills and top performance in times of change.

He received his undergraduate degree from Wheaton College and his doctorate in psychology from Northern Illinois University. Dr. Tim has written multiple books, including *The Coward's Guide to Conflict,* which is in its fourth printing and has been translated into six foreign languages. Other books include:

The Confidence Plan: How to Build a Stronger You

Coaching the Sale

The Top Performer's Guide to Conflict

The Top Performer's Guide to Change

The Top Performer's Guide to Speeches and Presentations

The Top Performer's Guide to Attitude

Tough Times Tactics

Soft Souls Living in a Harsh World

Dr. Tim is a frequent speaker on a variety of topics that benefit individuals in the workplace and personal life. He has been interviewed and featured in *The Wall Street Journal, The Bottom Line*, *The Chicago Tribune*, *People Magazine*, *Readers Digest*, *First for Women* and other periodicals. He has also appeared on *CNN radio news*, *VH-1 News*, *Total Living* and *ABC Channel 7 News*.

The Coaching Conversation

Carole Cowperthwaite-O'Hagan, RCC™, CACC

Energy, relationships, attention to detail, follow-through...these are the core terms most often used to describe Carole's passion for creating breakthrough strategies for her coachees. Her special focus has been the world of sales and marketing for over 20 years. With a background in manufacturing, financial services, professional services, retail and IT consulting, Carole brings a good cross section of marketing and management experience. A recognized expert for her work, Carole is a trainer, popular speaker and author and is known for her engaging presentations and creative training style. She has taught coaching techniques to hundreds of individuals, teams and groups within organizations across the country and internationally. Carole is a Registered Corporate Coach (RCC™) and lead instructor (RICC) for the Worldwide Association of Business Coaches (WABC). She is also a Certified Advanced Corporate Coach and Trainer (CACC). Carole is a co-author of the book *Tough Times Tactics: A Brief Practical Guide to De-stressing, Recharging and Focusing.*

The Coaching Conversation

Antoinette DuBois-Ayers, CPCC, RCC^{TM}

 Antoinette is a Certified Professional Co-Active Coach (CPCC), utilizing a style of coaching which actively involves the collaboration of both coachee and coach to help coachees achieve maximum results and sustain life-changing behavior in both their professional and personal lives. She brings over 25 years of experience, specializing in Leadership Development, Innovation, Team Productivity and Diversity. Her clients include Financial Services, Healthcare and Nonprofits. She is the co-developer of the Registered Corporate Coach (RCC^{TM}), the training program of the Worldwide Association of Business Coaches.

Top Achievements:
- Creator of a coaching clinic awarded national "Top 100" by Training Magazine
- Creator of a national African American Financial Advisor growth and productivity program
- Founder of Bridge Communications, a diversity engagement organization
- Led the formation of Community Health IT, a healthcare consortium
- Founded HLLC, a leading innovative healthcare model endorsed by the National Library of Medicine
- Founded the International Stillbirth Alliance

Made in the USA
Coppell, TX
27 January 2020